Perillo

P9-DEH-011

Adirondack Trails
CENTRAL
REGION

Third Edition
Forest Preserve Series, Volume III

Editor, Laurence T. Cagle
Series Editor, Neal Burdick

Adirondack Mountain Club, Inc.
Lake George, New York

Published by the Adirondack Mountain Club, Inc.
814 Goggins Road, Lake George, NY 12845-4117
www.adk.org

The Adirondack Mountain Club (ADK) is dedicated to the protection and responsible recreational use of the New York State Forest Preserve, parks, and other wild lands and waters. The Club, founded in 1922, is a member-directed organization committed to public service and stewardship. ADK employs a balanced approach to outdoor recreation, advocacy, environmental education, and natural resource conservation.

ADK encourages the involvement of all people in its mission and activities; its goal is to be a community that is comfortable, inviting, and accessible.

Library of Congress Cataloging-in-Publication Data

Adirondack trails. Central region / editor, Laurence T. Cagle.-- 3rd ed.
      p. cm. -- (Forest Preserve series ; v. 3)
   Rev. ed. of: Guide to Adirondack trails. Central region / by Bruce C.
   Wadsworth. 2nd ed.
c1994.
   Includes index.
   ISBN 1-931951-04-7 (pbk.)
 1. Hiking--New York (State)--Adirondack Mountains Region--Guidebooks. 2.
Adirondack Mountains Region (N.Y.)--Guidebooks. I. Cagle, Laurence T. II.
Wadsworth, Bruce. Guide to Adirondack trails. Central region. III. Adirondack
Mountain Club. IV. Series.
   GV199.42.N652A35 2003
   796.51'09747'5--dc22

                                 2003063948
ISBN: 1-931951-04-7 $19.95.—ISBN 1-931951-07-1 (set)

Printed in the United States of America
04 05 06 07 08 09 10   10 9 8 7 6 5 4 3 2 1

IN MEMORY OF

John Graves Cagle

1936–1987

Laurence T. Cagle

WE WELCOME YOUR COMMENTS

Use of the information in this book is at the sole discretion and risk of the hiker. Every effort has been made to keep this guidebook up-to-date; however, trail conditions are always changing.

In addition to reviewing the material in this book, hikers should assess their ability, physical condition, and preparation, as well as likely weather conditions, before a trip. For more information on preparation, equipment, and how to address emergencies, see the Introduction.

If you note a discrepancy in this book or wish to forward a suggestion, we welcome your comments. Please cite book title, year of most recent copyright and printing (see copyright page), trail, page number, and date of your observation. Thanks for your help!

Please address your comments to:

Publications
Adirondack Mountain Club
814 Goggins Road
Lake George, NY 12845-4117
518-668-4447, ext. 12
pubs@adk.org

EMERGENCIES

For all emergencies in Region 5, call the
Department of Environmental Conservation's
24-hour hotline: 518-891-0235

Contents

OVERVIEW MAPS   6,   7

PREFACE   9

INTRODUCTION   13

SIAMESE PONDS FROM THE SOUTH   31

SIAMESE PONDS FROM THE EAST   51

SIAMESE PONDS FROM THE NORTH   63

INDIAN LAKE SECTION   79

KUNJAMUK SECTION   101

WELLS TO LEWEY LAKE SECTION   109

BLUE MOUNTAIN LAKE SECTION   123

OLMSTEDVILLE-NEWCOMB SECTION   141

NORTHEAST SECTION   161

SOUTHEAST SECTION   171

APPENDICES

    I. Glossary of Terms   178

    II. State Campgrounds in or near the Central Region   179

ACKNOWLEDGMENTS   180

ABOUT THE EDITORS   182

ADIRONDACK MOUNTAIN CLUB   183

INDEX   188

Adirondack Park: Central Region

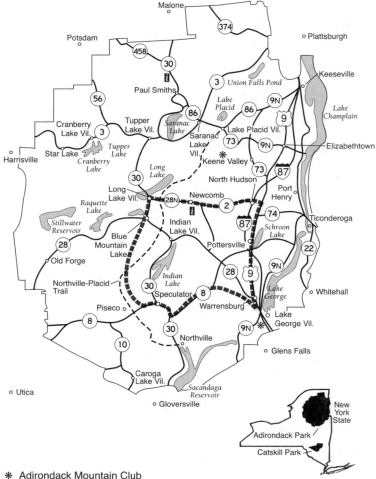

* Adirondack Mountain Club
🛈 Visitor Interpretive Center

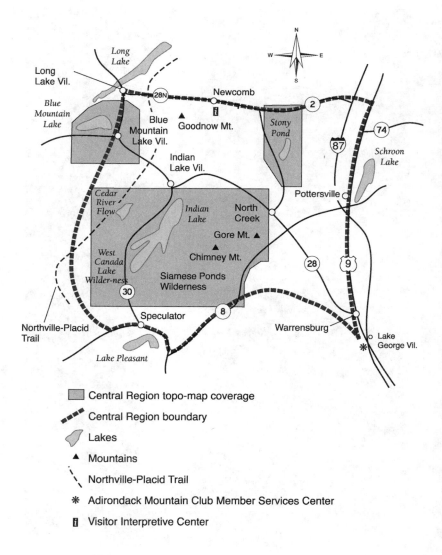

Central Region topo-map coverage

Central Region boundary

Lakes

▲ Mountains

Northville-Placid Trail

✳ Adirondack Mountain Club Member Services Center

🅸 Visitor Interpretive Center

Inlet to South Pond between Long and Blue Mountain Lakes.
PHOTOGRAPH BY MARK R. BOWIE

Preface

THE AREA COVERED BY THIS GUIDEBOOK is roughly bounded by the High Peaks to the north and Speculator to the south. The northern section between NY 28 and the High Peaks extends from Hoffman Notch on the east to the Sargent Ponds on the west. The section south of NY 28 extends west from NY 8 across the Siamese Ponds Wilderness and the Jessup River Wild Forest Area to the western edge of the Blue Ridge Wilderness and the Northville-Placid Trail in the West Canada Lake Wilderness. A small section between Warrensburg and Chestertown is included as well.

The Central Region's mountains are modest by High Peaks standards, although the highest, Snowy Mountain, misses the 4000-foot mark by only 101 feet. Nevertheless, a number of them are popular hiking destinations because of their outstanding views of the High Peaks, Indian or Blue Mountain lakes, ponds glittering in the sun, or mountains rolling off into the distance. Hordes of people climb to the caves and chimney-like rock formation on Chimney Mountain; fewer continue on to see the panoramic view from its true summit.

Apart from the mountains, the topography is predominantly rolling terrain and hiking is easy to moderate. This is a region of many lakes and ponds. By the New York State Department of Environmental Conservation's (DEC) count, there are thirty-six in or near the Siamese Ponds Wilderness alone. The Boreas, Cedar, Hudson, Indian, Jessup, Kunjamuk, Miami, and East Branch Sacandaga Rivers flow through the area. Altogether, the region's waterways provide many opportunities for canoeing and kayaking. From spring to fall, canoeists, kayakers, and literally hundreds of rafters, on their way from the Lake Abanakee Dam on the Indian River through the Hudson Gorge to North River, sweep by the beautiful Blue Ledges. But perhaps the most defining characteristic of the region, especially in the Siamese Ponds Wilderness, is the solitude that can be found in out-of-the-way places.

As with other areas in the Adirondacks, the region once was extensively logged. Here and there a few stands were spared the ax. A few miles north of Warrensburg, in the Charles Lathrop Pack Demonstration Forest, is the tallest recorded white pine in the state

(175 feet tall and at least 315 years old). International Paper Company (IP) still logs an area just north of Speculator, but the remaining forest has grown back. It supports a wide variety of plants and wildlife. In addition to an abundance of wildflowers and diverse species of hardwoods and conifers, hikers might see beaver dams and lodges, loons on secluded ponds, a white-tailed deer standing beside the trail, a partridge hen feigning injury to lure intruders away from her chicks, red squirrels scolding from pine trees, or the ubiquitous chipmunk. The black bear, bobcat, Eastern coyote, and moose inhabit the area, although the most that is likely to be seen of them are their tracks or scat along the trail.

Observant hikers will find ample evidence of the region's past, whether it be logging roads leading off into the deep woods, remains of logging camps, farm ruins near Curtis Clearing, foundations of a mansion and tannery near Fox Lair, the World War I garnet mine on Humphrey Mountain, or the old apple orchard at Burnt Shanty Clearing on the Siamese Ponds Trail. The Kunjamuk Trail, the trunk trail from NY 8 to Old Farm Clearing in the Siamese Ponds Wilderness, and the trail from Old Farm Clearing across to Puffer Ponds and Kings Flow formerly were stagecoach routes. The colorful trapper and guide Adirondack French Louie once trod the trail to Pillsbury Lake on his way to or from Speculator. There are seven fire towers still standing in the Central Region, although the future of the fire tower on Wakely Mountain, the tallest in the Forest Preserve, currently is being debated as part of the state's unit management planning process. (Fire tower aficionados might want to check out John P. Freeman's book *Views from on High: Fire Tower Trails in the Adirondacks and Catskills*, published by the Adirondack Mountain Club.)

But unquestionably the most famous incident in the region's past occurred during the night of September 13–14, 1901. President McKinley was shot by an anarchist in Buffalo on September 6 of that year. After being assured that the president was out of danger, Vice President Theodore Roosevelt undertook a trip to the Adirondacks. As he descended from Mount Marcy on the 13th, he received news that the president's condition had worsened. Not willing to wait for morning, Roosevelt left in the middle of the night on a hair-raising dash by horse and buckboard from Tahawus to the train station at North Creek, arriving at 4:39 A.M., only to find that President McKinley had died. Roosevelt had become president during the night.

All of the region's trails have been checked since the last ed[?] most have been remeasured with a surveyor's wheel. Ever[?] toring trails is a never-ending task. Readers need to be aware tha[?] conditions can change dramatically between editions, or even between printings. For example, the description of the Kunjamuk Trail across IP land has been revised twice since the last edition; first because logging roads had begun to grow in, and then again after IP reopened the route for logging operations. Logging operations also made access to the Kunjamuk Cave easier. The 1995 microburst closed off the upper end of the Extract Brook Trail; consequently, the trail description has been deleted. Other trails have become so overgrown in places that it is inadvisable to attempt them. For that reason, the Twin Ponds Path, Pine Hill Area Woods Walk, Wakely Brook to Round Pond Trail, and Whitney Lake Trail have been deleted; the Hoffman Notch to Big Pond Trail, which still appears on some DEC maps, should not be attempted as well. Every effort has been made to caution hikers about any remaining trails in danger of becoming overgrown wholly or partially.

In compensation for deleted trail descriptions, several new trail descriptions have been added since the previous edition. These include the Bullhead Pond, South Castle Rock, Blue Mountain Lake from South Castle Rock, Gore Mountain (Schaefer Trail), Big Bad Luck Pond, Ross Pond, and Whortleberry Pond trails.

Enjoy exploring the Central Region. As you pass through, please leave no trace.

—*Laurence T. Cagle*

Peaked Mountain.
PHOTOGRAPH BY CYNDI HESSE

Introduction

The Adirondack Mountain Club
Forest Preserve Series

The Forest Preserve Series of guides to Adirondack and Catskill trails covers hiking opportunities on the approximately 2.8 million acres of Forest Preserve (public) land within the Adirondack and Catskill Parks. The Adirondack Mountain Club (ADK) published its first guidebook, covering the High Peaks and parts of the Northville-Placid Trail, in 1934. In the early 1980s, coinciding with the decade-long centennial celebration of the enactment of the Forest Preserve legislation in 1885, ADK set out to achieve its long-time goal of completing a series of guides that would cover the two parks. Each guide in this series, listed below, is revised on a regular schedule.

Vol. 1:   *Adirondack Trails: High Peaks Region*
Vol. II: *Adirondack Trails: Northern Region*
Vol. III: *Adirondack Trails: Central Region*
Vol. IV: *Adirondack Trails: Northville-Placid Trail*
Vol. V: *Adirondack Trails: West-Central Region*
Vol. VI: *Adirondack Trails: Eastern Region*
Vol. VII: *Adirondack Trails: Southern Region*
Vol. VIII: *Catskill Trails*

The public lands that constitute the Forest Preserve are unique among all other wild public lands in the United States because they enjoy constitutional protection against sale or development. The story of this unique protection begins in the 1800s and continues today as groups such as ADK strive to guard it. This responsibility also rests with the public, who are expected not to degrade the Forest Preserve in any way while enjoying its wonders. The Forest Preserve Series of trail guides seeks not only to show hikers, skiers, and snowshoers where to enjoy their activities, but also to offer guidelines whereby users can minimize their impact on the land.

The Adirondacks

The Adirondack region of northern New York is unique in many ways. It contains the only mountains in the eastern United States that are not geologically Appalachian. In the late 1800s it was the first forested area in the nation to benefit from enlightened conservation measures. At roughly the same time it was also the most prestigious resort area in the country. In the twentieth century, the Adirondacks became the only place in the Western Hemisphere to host two winter Olympiads. In the 1970s the region was the first of significant size in the nation to be subjected to comprehensive land use controls. The Adirondack Forest Preserve (see below) is part of the only wild lands preserve in the nation whose fate lies in the hands of the voters of the entire state in which it is located.

Geologically, the Adirondacks are a southern appendage of the Canadian Shield. In the United States the Shield bedrock, which is over one billion years old, mostly lies concealed under younger rock, but it is well exposed in a few regions. Upward doming of the Adirondack mass in the past few million years—a process that is still going on, resulting in the mountains rising a few millimeters every century—is responsible for erosional stripping of the younger rock cover. The stream-carved topography has been extensively modified by the sculpting of glaciers, which, on at least four widely separated occasions during the Ice Age, completely covered the mountains.

Ecologically, the Adirondacks are part of a vegetation transition zone, with the northern, largely coniferous boreal forest (from the Greek god Boreas, owner of the north wind, whose name can be found on a mountain peak and a series of ponds in the High Peaks region) and the southern deciduous forest, exemplified by beech and maple stands, intermingling to present a pleasing array of forest tree species. Different vegetation zones are also encountered as one ascends the higher mountains in the Adirondacks; the tops of the highest peaks are truly arctic, with mosses and lichens that are common hundreds of miles to the north.

A rugged and heavily forested region, the Adirondacks were generally not hospitable to Native Americans, who used the region principally for hunting. Remnants of ancient campgrounds have been found in some locations. The native legacy survives principally in place names.

The first European to see the Adirondacks was likely the French explorer Jacques Cartier, who on his first trip up the St. Lawrence

River in 1535 stood on top of Mont Royal (now within the city of Montreal) and discerned high ground to the south. Closer looks were had by Samuel de Champlain and Henry Hudson, who came from the north and south, respectively, within a few weeks of each other in 1609.

For the next two centuries the Champlain Valley to the east of the Adirondacks was a battleground. Iroquois, Algonquin, French, British, and eventually American fighters struggled for control over the valley and with it supremacy over the continent. Settlers slowly filled the St. Lawrence Valley to the north, the Mohawk Valley to the south, and somewhat later the Black River Valley to the west. Meanwhile the vast, rolling forests of the interior slumbered in virtual isolation, disturbed only by an occasional hunter, timber cruiser, or wanderer.

With the coming of the nineteenth century, people discovered the Adirondacks. Virtually unknown as late as the 1830s (the source of the Nile River was located before the source of the Hudson River), by 1850 the Adirondacks made New York the leading timber producing state in the nation. This distinction did not last for long, though, as the supply of timber was quickly brought close to extinction. Meanwhile, mineral resources, particularly iron, were being exploited.

After the Civil War, people began to look toward the Adirondacks for recreation. At the same time, resource conservation and wilderness preservation ideas began to take hold, sometimes conflicting with the newfound recreational interests. Conservation and preservation concepts were given legal standing in 1885, when the New York State legislature created the Adirondack Forest Preserve and directed that "the lands now or hereafter constituting the Forest Preserve shall be forever kept as wild forest lands." This action marked the first time a state government had set aside a significant piece of wilderness for reasons other than scenic uniqueness.

In 1892, the legislature created the Adirondack State Park, consisting of Adirondack Forest Preserve land plus all privately owned land within a somewhat arbitrary boundary surrounding the Adirondacks, known as the "blue line" because it was drawn in blue on a large state map when it was first established. In 1894, in response to continuing abuses of the Forest Preserve law, the state's voters approved the inclusion of the "forever wild" portion of that law in the constitution of New York State, thus creating the only preserve in the nation that has constitutional protection. Today the Forest Preserve (those lands owned by the people of State of New York) consists of 2.4 million acres within the six-million-acre Adirondack Park, the largest park in the nation outside of Alaska.

After World War I, tourism gradually took over as the primary industry in the Adirondacks. The growth of the second-home industry spurred implementation of land use plans and an Adirondack Park Agency to manage them. While the plans and the Agency have remained controversial, they indicate the need to address the issues facing the Adirondacks boldly and innovatively.

Using This Guidebook

Like all the volumes in ADK Forest Preserve Series of guides to Adirondack trails, this book is intended to be both a reference tool for planning trips and a field guide to carry on the trail. Trails have been numbered consecutively and are located on the accompanying map by those numbers. Cross-referencing of trails is done by using the trail number.

Access to trails described in this book is from the Adirondack Northway (I-87) and US Route 9 on the east. The northern boundary of the region follows Blue Ridge Road from Exit 29 of the Northway westward to NY 28N, where it continues to Long Lake Village. NY 30 forms the western border from Long Lake until ten miles south of Speculator. The southern boundary follows NY 8 to Wevertown from NY 30; it then runs along NY 28 to the intersection with US 9 at Warrensburg. The eastern boundary then heads northward on US 9 to a point near Exit 29 of I-87.

Abbreviations and Conventions

In each of the books in the Forest Preserve Series, R and L, with periods omitted, are used for right and left. The R and L banks of a stream are determined by looking downstream. Likewise, the R fork of a stream is on the R when one faces downstream. N, S, E, and W, again without periods, are used for north, south, east, and west. Compass bearings are given in degrees. N is 0 degrees, E is 90 degrees, S is 180 degrees, and W is 270 degrees.

The following abbreviations are used in the text and on the maps:

ADK   Adirondack Mountain Club
APA   Adirondack Park Agency
DEC   New York State Department of Environmental Conservation

N-P	Northville-Placid (Trail)
PBM	Permanent Bench Mark
USGS	United States Geological Survey
4WD	four-wheel-drive vehicle
ft	feet
jct.	junction
km	kilometer or kilometers
m	meter or meters
mi	mile or miles
yd	yard or yards

Maps

The folded map enclosed in the back pocket of this book is a composite of USGS quadrangles with updated overlays of trails, shelters, and private land boundaries. A few isolated areas not shown on this map are shown on individual page maps located near the trail descriptions. See the map legend on page 18 for symbols used on the page maps.

The folded map is letter-number coded, with letters running across the top and bottom of the maps, and numbers running vertically on the sides (example: A4). Each trail's coordinate appears with the corresponding description in the book, and each trail is numbered on the map and in the book. These numbers are not used on any signs on the trail.

The USGS map quadrangles from which the composite map was made are the 15-minute series maps *Blue Mountain, Newcomb, Schroon Lake, Indian Lake,* and *Thirteenth Lake,* with additional information from the four-piece DEC Division of Lands and Forests' *Adirondack Map,* and the *Adirondack Park Preliminary Private Land Use and Development Plan Map* published by the Adirondack Park Agency. Extra copies of this map, *Trails of the Adirondack Central Region,* are available from ADK. It also is possible to obtain USGS 7.5-minute maps of this region.

Trail Signs and Markers

Marked and maintained DEC trails can be used by hikers, cross-country skiers, snowshoers, or even snowmobilers. Route descriptions include the color and type of trail marker. Blue markers generally indicate north-south trails; red markers generally indicate east-west trails; and yellow markers generally run at diagonal compass bearings.

One other type of marker is becoming more common. A yellow disk

Legend

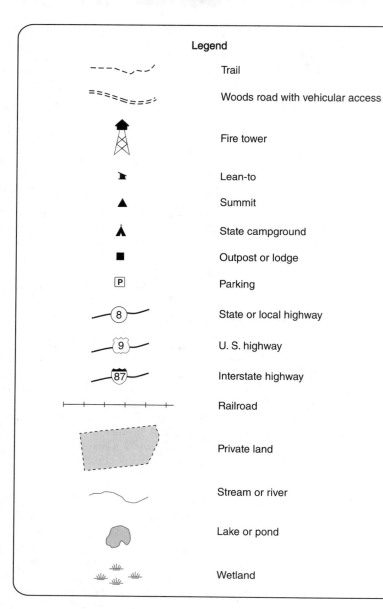

Trail

Woods road with vehicular access

Fire tower

Lean-to

Summit

State campground

Outpost or lodge

P Parking

8 State or local highway

9 U. S. highway

87 Interstate highway

Railroad

Private land

Stream or river

Lake or pond

Wetland

with a teepee on it indicates a designated camping area. A similar disk with an X through the teepee means one cannot camp at the location.

Snowmobile trail markers are larger than hiking, ski, and snowshoe trail markers. In recent years, the number of snowmobiles seen on the trails has diminished and skiers frequently use them, especially in the light-use midweek periods. Because ski, snowshoe, and snowmobile trails often cross marshland and river channels, they may be unsuitable for hiking in the summer months.

Well-used marked trails normally have trail signs located at the trailhead and all major trail junctions. These trail signs give the distance to named locations on the trail. In some cases, posted trail mileages may differ from distances provided in this book. ADK trail distances are measured using surveying wheels and other instruments, and in most cases are accurate.

The routes described in this book are normally not difficult to follow in the summer months. Winter travelers probably should keep within valley channels, unless on a well-marked trail. Many of the route descriptions offer optional extensions that can provide enjoyable challenge for those with the skills to pursue them.

Finally, it should go without saying that one should never remove any sign or marker. Hikers noticing damaged or missing signs should report this fact to the proper DEC offices at the addresses given below:

Hamilton County: Lands and Forests Headquarters
Department of Environmental Conservation
Northville, NY 12134
518-863-4545

Warren County: Lands and Forests Headquarters
Department of Environmental Conservation
Hudson Street Extension, P.O. Box 220
Warrensburg, NY 12885
518-623-3671

Essex County: Lands and Forests Headquarters
Department of Environmental Conservation
Ray Brook, NY 12977
518-897-1200

Access to many of the routes described in this guidebook is across private lands. Continued use of such private lands by the public is directly dependent upon the manner in which the public uses this land. The continued goodwill of public-spirited Adirondack landowners is dependent upon you and those in your hiking party. There may be "posted" signs at some points. These are usually to remind hikers that they are on private land over which the owner has kindly granted permission for hikers to pass. In most cases, leaving the trail, camping, fishing, and hunting are not permitted on these lands. Hikers should respect the owner's wishes.

Distance and Time

Care has been taken to be as accurate as possible in determining distances along trail routes. DEC has posted distances on marked trails; however, these have been verified and modified as needed by careful map review, use of professional survey measuring wheels, or, in some cases, use of a pedometer. Distances are expressed to the nearest tenth of a mile.

At the start of each section of this guide there is a list of trails in the region, the mileage unique to the trail, and the page on which the trail description begins. All mileages given in the trail description are cumulative, the beginning of the trail being the 0.0-mile point. A distance summary is given at the end of each description, with a total distance expressed in kilometers as well as in miles. If a trail has climbed significantly over its course, its total ascent in both feet and meters is provided.

To the inexperienced hiker, miles seem to vary in length depending on the weight of the pack, the hardness of the lean-to floor last night, the time of day, and whether one is walking uphill or downhill. The distances on old trail signs do not always reflect recent changes in trail routes or the presence of beaver dams that keep getting larger.

No attempt has been made to estimate travel time for these trails. A conservative rule to follow in estimating time is to allow an hour for every 1.5 miles, plus one-half hour for each 1000 feet of ascent, letting experience indicate how close the individual hiker is to this standard. Most day hikers will probably go a little faster than this, but backpackers will probably find they go somewhat slower. Some quickening of pace usually occurs when descending, though this may not be true on steep descents.

Wilderness Camping

It is not the purpose of this series to teach one how to camp in the woods. The information below should, however, serve to make hikers aware of the differences and peculiarities of the Adirondacks while giving strong emphasis to currently recommended procedures to reduce environmental damage—particularly in heavily used areas.

Except for Johns Brook Lodge, 3.5 miles up the Marcy Trail from Keene Valley (see *Adirondack Trails: High Peaks Region*), there are no huts in the Adirondacks for public use, such as are common in the White Mountains of New Hampshire. There are many lean-tos at convenient locations along trails and also many possibilities for tenting. The regulations regarding tenting and the use of lean-tos are simple and unrestrictive when compared to those of other popular backpacking areas in this country; but it is important that every backpacker know and obey the restrictions that do exist, since they are designed to

R. Loos

21

promote the long-term enjoyment and protection of the resource.

Except for groups of ten or more and smaller groups who wish to camp at one location for three nights or longer (see "Groups" below), no camping or fire permits are required in the Adirondacks, but campers must obey all DEC regulations regarding camping. Listed below are some of the most important regulations, which can also be found at http://www.dec.state.ny.us/website/dlf/publands/bacrule.htm.

Complete regulations are available from the DEC and are posted at most trail access points.

◆ Except where marked by a "Camp Here" disk, camping is prohibited within 150 feet of roads, trails, lakes, ponds, streams, or other bodies of water.

◆ Groups of ten or more persons or stays of more than three days in one place require a permit from the New York State Forest Ranger responsible for the area.

◆ Lean-tos are available in many areas on a first-come first-served basis. Lean-tos cannot be used exclusively and must be shared with other campers. (See also page 23.)

◆ Use pit privies provided near popular camping areas and trailheads. If none are available, dispose of human waste by digging a hole six to eight inches deep at least 150 feet from water or campsites. Cover with leaves and soil.

◆ Do not use soap to wash yourself, clothing, or dishes within 150 feet of water.

◆ Fires should be built in existing fire pits or fireplaces if provided. Use only dead and down wood for fires. Cutting standing trees is prohibited. Extinguish all fires with water and stir ashes until they are cold to the touch. Do not build fires in areas marked by a "No Fires" disk. Camp stoves are safer, more efficient, and cleaner.

◆ Carry out what you carry in. Use "leave no trace" practices.

◆ Keep your pet under control. Restrain it on a leash when others approach. Collect and bury droppings away from water, trails, and campsites. Keep your pet away from drinking water sources.

◆ Observe and enjoy wildlife and plants but leave them undisturbed.

◆ Removing plants, rocks, fossils, or artifacts from state land without a permit is illegal.

◆ Except in an emergency or between December 15 and April 30, camping is prohibited above an elevation of 4000 feet in the Adirondacks.

◆ Except in an emergency or between December 21 and March 21, camping is prohibited above an elevation of 3500 feet in the Catskills.
◆ At all times, only emergency fires are permitted above 4000 feet in the Adirondacks and 3500 feet in the Catskills.

Lean-tos

Lean-tos are available on a first-come, first-served basis up to the capacity of the shelter—usually about seven persons. Thus a small party cannot claim exclusive use of a shelter and must allow late arrivals equal use. Most lean-tos have a fireplace in front (sometimes with a primitive grill) and sanitary facilities. Most are located near some source of water, but each camper must use his or her own judgment as to whether or not the water supply needs purification before drinking. It is in very poor taste to carve or write one's initials in a shelter. Please try to keep these rustic shelters in good condition and appearance.

Since reservations cannot be made for any of these shelters, it is best to carry a tent or other alternate shelter. Many shelters away from the standard routes, however, are seldom used, and a small party can often find a shelter open in the more remote areas.

The following regulations apply specifically to lean-tos, in addition to the general camping regulations listed above:
◆ No plastic may be used to close off the front of a shelter.
◆ No nails or other permanent fastener may be used to affix a tarp in a lean-to, but it is permissible to use rope to tie canvas or nylon tarps across the front.
◆ No tent may be pitched inside a lean-to.

Groups

Any group of ten or more persons or smaller groups intending to camp at one location three nights or longer must obtain a permit before camping on state land. This system is designed to prevent overuse of certain critical sites and also to encourage groups to split into smaller parties more in keeping with the natural environment. Permits can be obtained from the DEC forest ranger closest to the actual starting point of one's proposed trip. The local forest ranger can be contacted by writing directly; if in doubt about whom to write, send the letter to the DEC Lands and Forests Division Office address for the county in which your trip will take place (refer to DEC addresses in Trail Signs and Markers section). They will forward the letter to the proper ranger, but write early enough to permit a response before your trip date.

One can also make the initial contact with the forest ranger by telephone. Keep in mind that the forest rangers' schedules during the busy summer season are often unpredictable. Forest rangers are listed in the white pages of local phone books under "New York, State of; Environmental Conservation, Department of; Forest Ranger." Bear in mind when calling that most rangers operate out of their private homes; observe the normal courtesy used when calling a private residence. Contact by letter is much preferred, and, as one can see, camping with a large group requires careful planning with a lead time of several weeks to ensure a happy, safe outing.

Forest Safety

The routes described in this guidebook vary from wide, well-marked DEC trails to narrow, unmarked footpaths that have become established through long use. With normal alertness and careful preparation the hiker should have few problems in land navigation. Nevertheless, careful map study and route planning are fundamental necessities. Hikers should never expect immediate help should an emergency occur. This is particularly true in winter, when fewer people are on the trails and weather is a larger factor.

In addition to a map, all hikers should carry a compass and know at least the basics of its use. In some descriptions, the Forest Preserve Series uses compass bearings to differentiate trails at a junction or to indicate the direction of travel above timberline. More important, a compass can be an indispensable aid in the event that you lose your way.

Winter trips, especially, must be carefully planned. Travel over ice on ski and snowshoe trips must be done with caution. The possibility of freez-

CELL PHONES

Cell phones should not be relied upon in case of emergency. Despite several highly publicized stories, their use in the mountains is limited by terrain, distance from communication towers, and other factors. Those who carry them should, out of consideration for their fellow backcountry users, use them only when necessary—and should have alternative plans for handling emergencies in case they do not operate.

ing rain, snow, and cold temperatures should be considered from early September until late May. True winter conditions can commence as early as November and last well into April, particularly at higher altitudes. It is highly recommended that hikers travel in parties of at least four people, be outfitted properly, rest when the need arises, and drink plenty of water. Leave trip plans with someone at home and then stick to your itinerary. For more information on winter travel, refer to the ADK publication *Winterwise* by John Dunn.

Drinking Water

For many years, hikers could trust practically any water source in the Adirondacks to be pure and safe to drink. Unfortunately, as in many other mountain areas, some Adirondack water sources have become contaminated with a parasite known as *Giardia lamblia*. This intestinal parasite causes a disease known as giardiasis—often called "beaver fever." It can be spread by any warm-blooded mammal when infected feces wash into the water; beavers are prime agents in transferring this parasite because they spend so much of their time in and near water. Hikers themselves have also become primary agents in spreading this disease since some individuals appear to be unaffected carriers of the disease, and other recently infected individuals may inadvertently spread the parasite before their symptoms become apparent.

PREVENTION: Follow the guidelines for the disposal of human excrement as stated in the section "Wilderness Camping" (page 28). Equally important, make sure that every member of your group is aware of the problem and follows the guidelines as well. The health of a fellow hiker may depend on your consideration.

WATER TREATMENT: No water source can be guaranteed to be safe. Boil all water for 2–3 minutes, utilize an iodine-based chemical purifier (available at camping supply stores and some drug and department stores), or use a commercial filter designed specifically for giardiasis prevention. If after returning from a trip you experience recurrent intestinal problems, consult your physician and explain your potential problem.

Hunting Seasons

One marvelous aspect of publicly owned land is that it is open to everyone for many recreational purposes, one of the most popular being hunting. Confrontations can occur when hikers and hunters are inconsiderate of the needs and rights of each other. Problems can be greatly reduced by careful planning.

It is advisable to avoid heavily hunted areas during big game seasons. Because it is difficult to carry a deer or bear carcass long distances or over steep terrain, hikers will find few hunters more than a mile from a roadway or in rugged mountain country. Lower slopes of beech, maple, and hemlock have much more hunting pressure than cripplebush, spruce, and balsam fir on upper slopes. Motorized vehicles are not allowed in areas designated as Wilderness, so hike there; most areas designated Wild Forest have woods roads where vehicles can be used, so avoid these areas, which are likely to be favored by hunters. Try to avoid the opening and closing days of regular deer season. For safety, wear a bright-colored outer garment; orange is recommended.

Big game seasons in the Adirondacks are usually as follows:

◆ Early Bear Season: Begins the first Saturday after the second Monday in September and continues for four weeks.
◆ Archery Season (deer and bear): September 27 to opening of the regular season.
◆ Muzzle-loading Season (deer and bear): The seven days prior to the opening of regular season.
◆ Regular Season: Next to last Saturday in October through the first Sunday in December.

On occasion, special situations require DEC to modify the usual dates of hunting seasons.

ADK does not promote hunting as one of its organized activities, but it does recognize that sport hunting, when carried out in compliance with the game laws administered by the DEC, is a legitimate sporting activity.

Bear Safety

Wildlife in the Adirondacks and Catskills can be a minor nuisance around a campsite.

Generally, the larger the animal the more timid it is in the presence of humans. The exception is the bear, which can be emboldened by the aroma of food.

The following tips will reduce the likelihood of an encounter with a bear:
◆ Never keep food in your tent or lean-to.
◆ DEC strongly encourages the use of bear-resistant canisters in the Eastern High Peaks Wilderness Area.
◆ In other areas, use a canister or hang food at least fifteen feet off the ground from a rope strung between two trees that are at least fifteen feet apart and 100 feet from the campsite.
◆ Wrap aromatic foods well.
◆ Wrap trash in sealed containers such as large Ziploc bags and hang or put in canister.
◆ Hang your pack, along with clothing worn during cooking.
◆ Keep a garbage-free fire pit away from your camping area.
◆ Should a bear appear, do not provoke it by throwing objects or approaching it. Bang pots, blow a whistle, shout, or otherwise try to drive it off with sharp noises. Should this fail, leave the scene.
◆ Report bear encounters to a forest ranger.

LEAVE NO TRACE

ADK supports the seven principles of the Leave No Trace program:

1. PLAN AHEAD AND PREPARE
♦ Know the regulations and special considerations for the area you'll visit.
♦ Prepare for extreme weather, hazards, and emergencies.
♦ Travel in groups of less than ten people to minimize impacts.

2. TRAVEL AND CAMP ON DURABLE SURFACES
♦ Hike in the middle of the trail; stay off of vegetation.
♦ Camp in designated sites where possible.
♦ In other areas, don't camp within 150 feet of water or a trail.

3. DISPOSE OF WASTE PROPERLY
♦ Pack out all trash (including toilet paper), leftover food, and litter.
♦ Use existing privies, or dig a cat hole five to six inches deep,
  then cover hole.
♦ Wash yourself and dishes at least 150 feet from water.

4. LEAVE WHAT YOU FIND
♦ Leave rocks, plants, and other natural objects as you find them.
♦ Let photos, drawings, or journals help to capture your memories.
♦ Do not build structures or furniture or dig trenches.

5. MINIMIZE CAMPFIRE IMPACTS
♦ Use a portable stove to avoid the lasting impact of a campfire.
♦ Where fires are permitted, use existing fire rings and only collect downed
  wood.
♦ Burn all fires to ash, put out campfires completely, then hide traces of fire.

6. RESPECT WILDLIFE
♦ Observe wildlife from a distance.
♦ Avoid wildlife during mating, nesting, and other sensitive times.
♦ Control pets at all times, and clean up after them.

7. BE CONSIDERATE OF OTHER VISITORS
♦ Respect other visitors and protect the quality of their experience.
♦ Let natural sounds prevail; avoid loud sounds and voices.
♦ Be courteous and yield to other users on the trail.

For further information on Leave No Trace principles log on to www.lnt.org.

Rabies Alert

Rabies infestation has been moving north through New York State. While it is most often associated with raccoons, any warm-blooded mammal can be a carrier.

Although direct contact with a rabid animal in the forest is not likely, some precautions are advisable:

◆ Do not feed or pet any wild animals, under any circumstances.
◆ Particularly avoid any wild animals that seem to be behaving strangely.
◆ If bitten by a wild animal, seek medical attention immediately.

Insect-Borne Diseases

While most insects can be at the worst annoying, in the areas covered in the ADK Forest Preserve Series of trail guides two carry potentially lethal diseases, particularly in the southern extremities of the coverage area (the Catskills). Deer ticks can spread Lyme disease, while mosquitoes can transmit West Nile virus.

In both instances, protection is advisable. Wear long pants and long-sleeved shirts and apply an insect repellent with the recommended percentage of DEET. On returning home, thoroughly inspect yourself and wash yourself and your clothing immediately. Seek immediate attention if any early symptoms (rash, long-term fatigue, headache, fever) arise.

Unmaintained Trails

Some trails are routinely maintained by DEC crews, forest rangers, ADK, or other designated groups and individuals. These trails are generally clear and otherwise in good condition, though seasonal blow-down, heavy storms, or other events may temporarily cause a trail problem. In this guidebook series, such trails are numbered both in the book and on its accompanying map.

Other trails have no designated maintainers. The hiker should not expect these trails to be in as good condition as the maintained trails. These unmaintained trails are described in the guidebooks, but are not numbered. The hiker should be prepared for a less clear route when using these trails. They are normally quite usable, unless otherwise noted in the guides. In some cases, undesignated maintainers such as hunters, anglers, or interested hikers have unofficially taken care of a trail. In this case the user may find the trail in good shape. However, the user of a trail defined as unmaintained in this guide should not expect this to be the case.

Should a trail become temporarily unclear, leave one person at the last known point of the trail, sending other hikers out in a fan pattern in all directions until the trail is relocated. All people must stay within sight and/or hearing distance of each other. Minor blowdowns are usually the cause of such circumstances.

Some routes are defined as bushwhacks—there is no trail. Sometimes, frequent use of the bushwhack route produces one or more "herd paths," which may or may not lead to the desired destination. Bushwhackers should have good map navigation skills and should have done thorough planning before initiating the outing. Careful selection of party members for experience, skills, and physical condition can decrease the chance of problems. It is always a good idea to have extra food and be prepared for the "unexpected" night in the woods. Carry suitable first-aid gear. Be sure someone at home knows your specific area of hiking and when and how to inform DEC if you have not returned on schedule. ◆

Siamese Ponds
FROM THE SOUTH

Trails in this section all enter the Siamese Ponds Wilderness Area from NY 8. This area of the Forest Preserve of over 108,000 acres has 36 ponds and lakes, primarily draining into the East Branch Sacandaga River. Elevations range from 1280 ft to 3472 ft. Most grades are gradual, following water tributaries through their valleys.

Access to NY 8 from the W in this section is off NY 30, 3.0 mi N of Wells. From the E, drive SW on NY 8 from Wevertown, where it crosses NY 28.

The SW part of the Siamese Ponds Wilderness Area is one of the last truly remote portions of the Forest Preserve. Only hunters' and anglers' trails probe up the tributaries of the East Branch Sacandaga River, leaving the interior a true wilderness. The most used marked trail described in this chapter is the East Branch Sacandaga Trail. It is a trunk trail for several other trails in the region.

This is a region where hiking is enjoyable, fishing is good, and wildlife is plentiful. Since many of the trails are unmarked hunters' paths, hikers should study their maps well and carry a compass.

Following are some recommended hikes in this section:

SHORT HIKES
- Auger Falls: 2.6 mi (4.2 km) round trip. A hike along an old woods road to a charming waterfall.
- East Branch Sacandaga Gorge and Square Falls: 2.4 mi (3.9 km) round trip. An unmarked footpath leads through a narrow gorge to a small waterfall and swimming hole.

MODERATE HIKES
- Shanty Brook and Mud Ponds: 7.6 mi (12.3 km) round trip. Shanty Brook is a pleasant trail through the forest to two attractive bodies of water.
- Second Pond: 5.4 mi (8.7 km) round trip. Rolling terrain and open forests make a delightful trip to an attractive lake.

HARDER HIKES:

- ◆ Siamese Ponds: 4.6 mi (7.4 km) round trip. A variety of conditions ranging from crossing a ridge to strolling along the East Branch makes for a longer day than intended.
- ◆ Curtis Clearing: 3.4 mi (5.5 km) round trip. A bit of careful observation necessary to find your way into one of the least traveled parts of the region.

TRAIL DESCRIBED	TOTAL MILES (one way)	PAGE
Auger Falls (East Side)	1.3 (2.1 km)	32
County Line Brook	4.8 (7.7 km)	33
Shanty Brook and Mud Ponds	3.8 (6.1 km)	36
Fox Lair Walk	1.0 (1.6 km)	39
East Branch Sacandaga Gorge and Square Falls	1.2 (1.9 km)	40
East Branch Sacandaga to Old Farm Clearing	9.6 (15.5 km)	41
Curtis Clearing	1.7 (2.7 km)	43
Siamese Ponds	2.3 (3.7 km)	44
Bog Meadow	2.5 (4.0 km)	45
Second Pond	2.7 (4.4 km)	46
Gore Mt. (Schaefer Trail)	4.5 (7.3 km)	47

(1) **Auger Falls Trail** (East Side)

Map: Page 34

The hike to Auger Falls can be expanded many ways to make a delightful day hike. The falls is unusual. Its twisting course among rugged boulders and cliffs is intriguing.

▶ Trailhead: Access is off NY 8 at the abandoned village of Griffin. From the jct. of NY 8 and NY 30, N of Wells, proceed 2.6 mi NE along NY 8. At this point, there is a DEC signpost for Old Pine Orchard and Macomber Creek. Across the road to the L is a dirt road (easy to miss). The bridge over the East Branch Sacandaga River 0.2 mi down the dirt road has been reopened to vehicular traffic, but parking on the opposite side of the bridge is limited and access to private camps should not be restricted. Ample parking is available near NY 8. The trail bears L once across the bridge. ◀

FROM THE BRIDGE (0.0 mi), a gently rolling narrow dirt road heads W. At 0.5 mi, it passes a camp on the L. Red snowmobile markers begin at a barrier gate immediately beyond the camp. The old road becomes a grassy lane through a mixed wood forest.

At 1.3 mi, a DEC warning sign on a tree states, "Warning—Hazardous Gorge Area—Sheer Cliffs—Swift Water—Slippery Footing." A side trail L leads to the river above Auger Falls. Informal paths branch off from this trail and head downstream to the falls. Good views of the cascading water are found from the paths that wind along the top of the cliffs above the water. Hikers are encouraged to be careful.

The trip can be extended by continuing along the old road. It is well worth considering, since the route is very attractive. Macomber Creek is reached at 1.5 mi. (A bushwhack up this creek provides another way into the extremely wild southern portion of the Siamese Ponds Wilderness Area.) A snowmobile bridge crosses the creek.

The route soon becomes a grassy footpath along the river. It then bears R, away from the water, gaining slight elevation. Lush ferns make the next half-mile extremely nice. Beyond this point, leased land of the International Paper Co. is found; it is not open for hiking by the general public.

Upon the return to the bridge over the East Branch at Griffin, a short trip to Griffin Falls is in order. Cross the bridge (heading toward NY 8) and follow the road around a bend. At a large boulder R, a very steep informal path drops down the bank to the river and Griffin Falls. High cliffs border the falls. The raging water forces its way through sharply angular layers of rock. It is a geologist's dream spot. This is a perfect place to take photos or to have lunch.

❋ Trail in winter: Excellent cross-country skiing is possible along the old road described in this trip. For another trip, the skier can also continue 3.0 mi E of NY 8 to the virgin pines at Old Pine Orchard near Wells.

❧ Distances: To camp, 0.5 mi; to side trail (Auger Falls), 1.3 mi (2.1 km); to Macomber Creek, 1.5 mi (2.4 km).

(2) County Line Brook Trail

Map: E4–F4

County Line Brook roughly parallels the boundary line between Hamilton County and Warren County. The footpath along its W bank follows an old woods road to its terminus far back in the hills of the

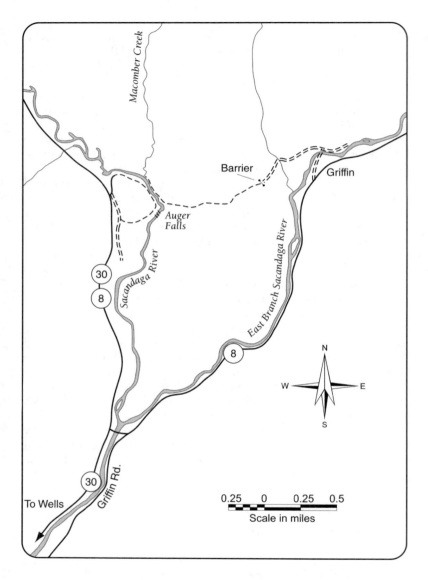

Auger Falls Trails (Trails 1, 40)

Siamese Ponds Wilderness Area. The variation in scenery makes this a very pleasant day hike.

▶ Trailhead: Access to the footpath is off NY 8, 0.2 mi SW of the Hamilton-Warren County boundary line road signs. There is a small pullout on the R. A steep path drops off the bank 50 ft down to the East Branch Sacandaga River. A short way downstream, two cables span the river. However, it is easier to rock-hop to the opposite bank by going slightly upstream. The County Line Brook footpath begins on the opposite bank at the cables (0.0 mi). A large DEC "Rules and Regulations" sign is nailed to a tree at this point. There is a fire ring nearby. ◀

THE FOOTPATH LEADS inland from the river approximately 100 yd, where it intersects another path. Turn R (NE), and follow this path. County Line Brook is reached at 0.2 mi, just upstream from its confluence with the East Branch. A single cable crosses County Line Brook here. The path now parallels the brook's W bank along a well-defined woods road running N.

The route moves back from the brook after a few minutes. At 0.8 mi, a long grade climbs high above the brook, which continues to be visible downslope. Eventually, the gradient of the brook brings it up to the path's elevation.

The trail reaches a vlei at 2.0 mi. The sizeable outlet stream of Buckhorn Pond cuts across the path. (County Line Brook Falls is near here. Turn around and walk back along the path until you are on dry ground at the edge of the wet area. Then walk 200 yd E into the woods, staying on dry ground along the edge of the vlei to the falls. The falls drops 7 ft into a deep pool. This is a nice place to swim.) The path skirts the vlei on higher dry ground. To the R, the vlei is studded with small beaver dams, alders, and open stretches. Both the route and the change of scenery are pleasant.

The trail gradually moves away from the brook, but after dropping down a short grade at 2.5 mi comes alongside the brook again at the jct. of its E and W branches. The E branch extends toward Mud Ponds to the NE, while the W branch heads N and then NW. The brook runs wide and deep here.

As the trail continues along the W branch, at 2.6 mi a huge erratic can be seen to the L. A single cable crosses the brook at 3.1 mi. The stream is noticeably more narrow and rocky; the valley more closed in. The route is beside the brook, occasionally moving away from and then returning to the water.

The trail comes to Lost Creek at 3.7 mi. The 1990 USGS *Bakers Mills* map shows the trail ending here. The path is lightly used beyond this point and inexperienced hikers might consider turning around. The trail parallels the W bank of the brook to a large clearing; so long as that is remembered and the brook is kept within sight or sound, the chances of getting lost are very slim.

A large beaver dam is on the R at 4.0 mi. Almost immediately, the path changes direction sharply, looping W in a horseshoe before heading NW again.

At 4.3 mi, the valley narrows considerably and the grade becomes moderate. The route climbs away from the stream on an eroded section of the old road and soon the sound of a rushing stream is noted. A brief side trip will reveal that the brook's course falls through a narrow, deep, vertical rock gorge.

Height of land at 4.6 mi features another vlei. The slowly moving water is in a deep channel. The trail crosses another small tributary near the end of this attractive vlei at 4.7 mi, then passes through the forest to a clearing at 4.8 mi. Here there is an old hunters' campsite. A large set of tiered bunks stood in the open in 1998, an incongruous sight deep in the woods.

✳ Trail in winter: The County Line Brook footpath has ideal grades and width for cross-country skiing. It makes a nice day trip or can be combined with the Shanty Brook–Mud Ponds Trail (trail 3) for a very rugged outing. As with many NY 8 trails, one must find a frozen ice bridge across the East Branch before it is possible to enjoy a winter outing.

🐾 Distances: To County Line Brook, 0.2 mi; to long grade, 0.8 mi; to vlei, 2.0 mi; to jct. of E and W branches, 2.5 mi; to Lost Creek, 3.7 mi; to height of land, 4.6 mi; to clearing at end of trail, 4.8 mi (7.7 km).

(3) Shanty Brook and Mud Ponds Trail

Map: E5–F5

The hike up Shanty Brook into the Mud Ponds region is a trip into one of the most beautiful sections of the Siamese Ponds Wilderness Area. The grades are negligible. As in all unmarked trail travel, the hiker should carry and use both map and compass.

In the heyday of guiding in the Adirondacks, many of the nicest bodies of water were unfortunately called Mud Pond or Mud Lake. There are over thirty such bodies of water in the mountains with this unin-spiring appellation. It is said this was done by the guides themselves, to make other guides believe those ponds were not good for fishing. The ponds in this case should perhaps have been called the Blue Hills Lakes to do them justice. They are jewels in the forest.

▶ Trailhead: Access is from NY 8 at the large DEC Shanty Brook parking area. This is 10.1 mi NE of the jct. of NY 8 and NY 30 N of Wells and 4.7 mi SW of the large parking area at the Siamese Ponds Wilderness Area trailhead. ◀

A DIRT ROAD SLANTS L (NW), from NY 8 toward the East Branch Sacandaga River, slightly more than 0.1 mi N of the parking area. About 100 ft along this road, several rough paths lead down a steep bank to the water's edge. Here, two single cables stretch across the river. They mark the start of the Shanty Brook footpath on the oppo-site bank (0.0 mi). This is downstream from the place where Shanty Brook enters the East Branch. At times of low water in the summer and fall, the East Branch is wide but very shallow at this point. Rock-hop or wade across the stream.

Climb the opposite bank and locate the beginning of the path. It is well traveled and easy to follow. It soon heads inland away from the river in a generally N direction. The path reaches the W bank of Shanty Brook at 0.2 mi and follows it for a short distance. The route then angles up a slope away from the water, though you can still see the brook for a while. At 0.7 mi, a 75 ft long wet section is reached, where you cannot see the brook. The trail bends just beyond this point.

Approximately 100 yd into the woods to the R (E), Shanty Brook Falls is located. A faint path leads to the falls. The water tumbles over a 12 ft rock ledge into a deep pool below. The stream cuts through the sheer walls of the gorge as it flows downstream. This is a lovely spot and an ideal place for a swim. Extremely interesting curves and cuts through the rock channel are visible for a long distance upstream from the falls.

Returning to the main trail, the route continues N. The path makes a brief swing E at 1.3 mi, crosses a rocky tributary brook, and then cross-es to the E side of Shanty Brook at 1.4 mi. For the next half-mile, the sounds of the gurgling brook entertain you as you walk along its E side.

A large but somewhat empty vlei is reached at 1.9 mi. There is some evidence beaver may be returning to fill the vlei again. The Blue Hills ridge is to the W; Black Mt. can be glimpsed over the trees to the NE. Stay to the E side of the vlei and head in a straight line to its NE corner. Here, the path becomes obvious again.

After another short wet section, the valley begins to narrow down against the ridge L. The brook cuts between the path and the ridge, but is not generally visible. The vlei becomes a series of beaver meadows, visible L.

The path continues N until it is along Shanty Brook again. A large beaver meadow at 2.7 mi is where Stockholm Brook merges with Shanty Brook. Big Hopkins Mt. can be seen in the distant NE.

Cross Shanty Brook on the large rocks at the edge of the meadow. Once across, find the narrow rock channel that runs along the W edge of the meadow. Follow it until you pick up the faint path that continues along the edge of the meadow. Continue to the NW edge of the meadow, where the trail again becomes easy to follow. It angles upward away from the meadow.

The path swings W at 2.8 mi. The low, rolling terrain is easy to walk and the trail is obvious.

The E end of the first Mud Pond is reached at 3.5 mi. The path extends along its S shore. A prominent rock formation can be seen across the pond at its midpoint. Open campsites are found at the midpoint and at the far end of the pond.

The footpath winds over a small ridge at the end of the lake and terminates at 3.8 mi. Here a huge beaver dam divides the two ponds. Gigantic logs have drifted up against the dam. They provide an ideal spot to sit and eat lunch.

The view W down the second Mud Pond is one of the best in the Siamese Ponds Wilderness Area. Nearly a half-mile of water pierces the forest here. Buckhorn Mt., with Macomber Mt. behind its R shoulder, completes the scene.

❊Trail in winter: In late winter, when the East Branch Sacandaga is frozen over, this is a fine cross-country trip. Follow the trail to the first vlei and then ski right up snow-covered Shanty Brook to the Mud Ponds. Good map navigators then ski the ponds, swing SW around the Blue Hills, and ski down County Line Brook's E branch back to NY 8. This trip requires good backcountry skiing capabilities.

🐾 Distances: To Shanty Brook, 0.2 mi; to Shanty Brook crossing, 1.4 mi; to vlei, 1.9 mi; to fork, 2.5 mi; to beaver meadow, 2.7 mi; to first Mud Pond, 3.5 mi; to end of trail, 3.8 mi (6.1 km).

Fox Lair Walk (unmaintained)

Map: E5

Fox Lair is the name Alexander Hudnut gave his estate, which is now state property. Its ruins, along with those of the old Oregon Tannery, provide points of interest for a short walk of up to a mile over the roads and paths of this land. It is a good place for a stroll, lunch, and a swim in the East Branch.

▶ Trailhead: The N end of the estate is accessed via two dirt roads that head W across a meadow 2.2 mi SW of the Siamese Ponds Wilderness Area parking lot and 2.5 mi NE of the Shanty Brook parking area on NY 8. At the S end, a grassy road slants toward the river 3.0 mi SW of the Siamese Ponds Wilderness Area parking lot and 1.7 mi NE of the Shanty Brook parking area. The grassy road is within eyesight of a more obvious pullout and a dirt road that dead-ends a few yards into the woods. ◀

BOTH RUINS are most easily found from the S end. A faint trail drops down the bank L toward the river about 100 yd from the rock barrier across the grassy road. The remains of the tannery can be found in the undergrowth. Continuing on, the grassy road soon passes steps leading down to a swimming hole L and then a more elaborate set of steps heading obliquely R up a knoll to the Fox Lair ruins.

The hiker who enjoys a bit more challenge can find the Fox Lair ruins from the N end of the estate by following a dirt road paralleling NY 8 until it turns into a grassy path. After crossing two old bridges with iron railings, a search through the undergrowth toward the river will reveal the knoll and ruins.

❉ Trail in winter: Winter use of the area could be fun, especially as a beginning snowshoe outing for children. Stay away from the river ice however.

🐾 Distance: Approximately 1.0 mi (1.6 km).

East Branch Sacandaga Gorge and Square Falls Trail

(unmaintained)   Map: E5

This exquisite little trip is for the nimble-footed and light at heart. The camera buff will find it fascinating; the lover of wildflowers will not be disappointed. The trip is best done in summer or fall, when the water of the East Branch is low. The water is swift and your rock-hopping skills must not fail you, if you wish to stay dry.

▶ Trailhead: Access is off NY 8, where an unmarked abandoned dirt road angles NW into the woods toward the East Branch. This dirt road is 1.9 mi S of the large DEC parking area at the Siamese Ponds Wilderness Area trailhead and 2.8 mi N of the DEC Shanty Brook parking area. There is a wide, sandy shoulder at the N end of a small grassy field where the road begins (0.0 mi). ◀

THE WINDING ROAD dead-ends at 0.1 mi. A path extends onward a short distance to a crossing of a small stream. On the opposite side, the path heads L for 20 yd and then abruptly turns R and climbs a little grade. A few more yards of travel and the East Branch can be seen L below. The route continues N (upstream). The trail splits briefly, but soon rejoins.

At 0.3 mi, a side trail branches L 30 yd to the rocky riverbank, where a double cable stretches across the creek. (It is for use in times of high water, but is a very risky venture at best.) Go upstream until you find a suitable spot to rock-hop to the opposite bank.

Once across the stream, climb to the top of the riverbank. Find the informal path that heads upstream. Beautiful large hemlocks give shade as you gaze down into the rock-walled gorge.

The valley wall steepens greatly at 0.5 mi. While there is no significant difficulty, it is clear that one should not rush through the next section. The path contours the slope. Walk carefully.

The gorge widens again at 0.8 mi. The remainder of the trip is relatively flat and easy to walk. Square Falls at 1.2 mi, while not high, is quite broad. Water spills over the crest at several points, channeling into a deep pool at its base. It is a rare person who can resist a swim here.

Myriad wildflowers are found along the bank of the stream. A short walk beyond the falls is an immersion in lush ferns and flowers. Plan to spend some time here before the short return trip.

❄ Trail in winter: This is not a good winter route; the river and grades are not easy on snowshoes in places.

🐾 Distances: To side trail, 0.3 mi; to falls, 1.2 mi (1.9 km).

(4) East Branch Sacandaga Trail to Old Farm Clearing Trail

Map: B5–D5

This truck trail is the primary DEC trail into the Siamese Ponds Wilderness Area from the S. It runs NW to the beginning of the Siamese Ponds Trail (trail 5) and then swings N to Old Farm Clearing near Thirteenth Lake. Once you have climbed the shoulder of Eleventh Mt., the trail follows the old stagecoach route from North Creek to Bakers Mills for most of its course.

The East Branch Sacandaga Trail is often used by hikers, skiers, and snowshoers for through trips with a car waiting for them at the other end of the trail. The trail description running in the opposite direction (from Old Farm Clearing, trail 14) can be found in the Siamese Ponds from the East Section.

▶ Trailhead: The trailhead is located on the W side of NY 8, 4.0 mi W of Bakers Mills. A large parking area, trail sign, and trail register are found here. ◀

THE TRAIL LEAVES the rear of the parking area, passes a trail register, and quickly steepens. Elevation increases 240 ft before the col across the ridge of Eleventh Mt. at 0.3 mi. Here, the old stagecoach route enters from the L and the grade moderates. Walking is level through the col, but steepens again as you start the descent on the far side of the ridge. Views of the cliffs of Eleventh Mt. on the R are interesting.

A long, gradual descent brings you to Diamond Brook at 1.5 mi. (Diamond Brook intersects the Bog Meadow Trail 3.5 mi to the N.) This tributary of the East Branch is both shallow and broad. Spring freshets sometimes wash out the bridge here, but it generally isn't needed in the summer. These washouts may also make the trail unclear. Once across the brook, walk downstream several yards to the confluence with the East Branch. Here the trail is clear again, following the river upstream along its N bank.

A beaver meadow is soon reached, from which Diamond Mt. can be viewed to the N. The trail is essentially level here and closely parallels the river. Farther on, it alternately wanders away from the river and back again. A ford across the river to the Curtis Clearing Trail (page 43) at 2.6 mi is followed by Burnt Shanty Clearing at 2.7 mi. A few apple trees growing here are all that is left to indicate where the clearing once existed.

Still on the level, the trail moves farther from the river, coming to a trail jct. at 3.5 mi. The newer marked trail heads L toward the East Branch; the R fork is the original trail. A lean-to and a suspension bridge across the East Branch are reached at 4.0 mi. (The trail across the suspension bridge leads 2.3 mi to the Siamese Ponds; see trail 5.) From the lean-to, the trail heads upstream beside the E bank of the river. It rejoins the original trail at 4.3 mi.

At Big Shanty Flow, at 4.6 mi, a large, rustic sign on a tree states, "Big Shanty River Driving Camp 1890s." A large boulder R of the trail at 5.2 mi has a USGS benchmark in its center at eye level. The trail passes the cut made by Cross Brook on a bridge wide enough for skiers at 5.7 mi. The route crosses a much shallower East Branch section at 6.6 mi. A single-strand cable was once here, but a new bridge, suitable for skiing, was completed in 1992. The stream is easily rock-hopped at low-water periods. About 200 ft of elevation will be gained between here and Old Farm Clearing. At 7.7 mi, the trail begins to ascend, alternately climbing moderate and more gradual grades. It peaks at 8.8 mi, levels, and then gradually descends.

The marked trail from Kings Flow and Puffer Pond (trail 16) enters from the L at 9.5 mi. There is a signpost at this jct. A small spring on the R at 9.6 mi announces that the large clearing at Old Farm Clearing is just ahead.

❄ Trail in winter: For good skiers this is an excellent ski trail. Arranging vehicles for a through trip is time-consuming. Some short stretches require good control. Most people prefer skiing this trail from N to S.

🚶 Distances: To col, 0.3 mi; to Diamond Brook, 1.5 mi; to Curtis Clearing ford, 2.6 mi; to lean-to fork, 3.5 mi; to East Branch lean-to, 4.0 mi; to Big Shanty Flow, 4.6 mi; to Cross Brook, 5.4 mi; to East Branch crossing, 6.6 mi; to Puffer Pond Trail jct., 9.5 mi; to Old Farm Clearing, 9.6 mi (15.5 km). It is another 1.2 mi to summer parking area at east access point.

Curtis Clearing Trail (unmaintained)

Map: D5

Curtis Clearing is the site of an abandoned farm. There is little reason for going there, except to muse over occasional artifacts as you wander around the clearing. Getting there is the interesting part. If you wish to be in a little-traveled forest, where evidence of bears is much more abundant than evidence of humans, you'll enjoy this trip.

▶ Trailhead: Access is from the East Branch Sacandaga Trail (trail 4) starting at NY 8. The Curtis Clearing Trail follows a well-defined old woods road. Once located, it is easy to hike. Some care is required to locate it. ◀

THE HIKER LEAVES the East Branch Sacandaga Trail 2.6 mi from NY 8. This is 1.1 mi from the Diamond Brook Bridge. After being close to the East Branch for several minutes, this level trail edges away from and out of sight of the river. In a shallow dip, a small section of corduroy is crossed. Approximately 100 paces beyond this point is a large old blaze on a tree at the R side of the trail. "CC" is carved on the opposite side of the tree. This is where you must leave the East Branch Trail (0.0 mi). (Burnt Shanty Clearing is 0.1 mi farther on, with several old apple trees.)

Turning L, follow a faint path 200 ft to the bank of the East Branch. Two cables stretch across the river at this point (1997). Large rock formations are on both sides of the river here. A small sandbar and a very large gray birch are on the opposite side of the stream. Rock-hop or ford the river. The Curtis Clearing Trail begins on the opposite bank and heads W upstream.

At 0.1 mi, turn L, staying E of and above a marshy area near the river. Soon an old woods road is visible heading SW. The road is generally clear from this point to Curtis Clearing. The level route passes through mostly deciduous forest.

After crossing a brook at 0.3 mi, the path passes through a tiny circular clearing at 0.7 mi before heading W again. Soon thereafter it parallels Curtis Brook above its E bank. The route crosses Curtis Brook at the outlet of a large beaver meadow and pond at 1.0 mi. (The road is easier to find if the lower of the two beaver dams is used.) Sharply turning NW, the path curves around the beaver meadow. Turning W again, it heads up a long gradual grade.

At height of land the first of several large rock piles is seen. Soon after, the path reaches the first of several small clearings that comprised the Curtis Clearing farm. It continues beyond for 0.3 mi and ends in another old clearing. This is 1.7 mi from the East Branch.

❅ Trail in winter: Once across the river this trail could be an interesting part of a day's outing.

⚮ Distances: To East Branch, 200 ft; to Curtis Brook, 1.0 mi; to end of trail, 1.7 mi (2.7 km). Total distance from NY 8, 4.3 mi (6.9 km).

(5) Siamese Ponds Trail

Map: D4–D5

Siamese Ponds makes a good day's hike from NY 8 or an interesting exploration if one is camped at the lean-to on the East Branch Sacandaga River.

▶ Trailhead: The Siamese Ponds Trail begins at the lean-to where the suspension bridge crosses the East Branch Sacandaga River (0.0 mi). It is reached via the side trails to the lean-to from the East Branch Sacandaga Trail (trail 4). The lean-to and trailhead are 4.0 mi from NY 8 and 5.7 mi from Old Farm Clearing. The course of the trail is over the N shoulder of Siamese Mt., ascending 525 ft before reaching the ponds. ◀

FROM THE SUSPENSION BRIDGE the trail heads W. Beaver have been active R of the trail but their effects won't interfere with your hiking. At 0.4 mi the grade begins to increase.

The trail crosses Siamese Brook at 1.1 mi and reaches height of land at 2.1 mi. Here the trail descends briefly. It passes informal campsites, both L and R, at 2.2 mi before the final drop to the lower pond shoreline at 2.3 mi.

Paths have been made by anglers and hikers around both sides of the ponds. The most actively used one crosses a small beaver dam and skirts the S shoreline. It eventually reaches the upper pond after another 1.3 mi.

❅ Trail in winter: For those adept in backcountry skiing, Siamese Ponds makes a long trip but a very interesting place to visit.

⚮ Distances: To Siamese Brook, 1.1 mi; to height of land, 2.1 mi; to lower Siamese Pond, 2.3 mi (3.7 km). Total distance from NY 8, 6.3 mi (10.2 km).

(6) **Bog Meadow Trail**

The route follows a 180-year-old woods road over gentle grades and level stretches. The destination is an exquisite bog meadow where a rippling brook provides a very enjoyable lunch spot. In recent years, maintenance decline and summer growth have made this trail sometimes difficult to use. In places, nettles make long trousers a must. Most of the trail is obvious; however, a few places in the early part of the trip require care. Take a compass and map and remember that the course is generally W.

▶ Trailhead: To reach the trailhead, turn N off NY 8 onto Edwards Hill Rd. in the hamlet of Bakers Mills. Travel 1.5 mi, then pass on the L a large red farmhouse, a second red home, and finally a white house. The hike begins at a narrow unmarked road on the L, immediately past the white house (0.0 mi). Park cars on the shoulder of Edwards Hill Rd., beyond this point. ◀

FOLLOW THE ACCESS ROAD 0.1 mi over private land to a point where it begins to curve toward a white summer home. Here, the hiking route branches L onto a grassy woods road.

You soon pass an old log cabin and a well. At 0.3 mi, avoid a L turn with a chain barrier. Continue straight ahead on the less-used grassy path. Five minutes more walking brings you to denser forest and soon thereafter to state Forest Preserve land.

A gentle grade winds its way upward through the woods. Avoid a side trail R at 0.7 mi. At 1.0 mi, height of land is reached, 370 ft above the trailhead. Partway down the next slope, a tree on the R contains the mysterious carving "WVH DIED HERE OCT 1979." About 100 ft beyond the tree, the road turns L, and the Bog Meadow Trail continues straight ahead (NW) over a small hump of land.

A gradual descent then brings you to Diamond Brook at 1.3 mi. The trail angles L across the brook. From this point onward the route becomes much easier to follow. Conifers are numerous and the trail is level.

Ten minutes later a low ridge comes into view R and soon thereafter the land begins to drop off on the L. The trail continues at a gradual decline, leveling just before reaching Round Pond Brook and Bog Meadow at 2.5 mi. An open campsite is just across the brook, upstream from the meadow.

A walk on the meadow is impressive. The dense forest surrounds it;

45

SIAMESE PONDS FROM THE SOUTH

the brook meanders through it. The trail circles around the meadow and crosses Round Pond Brook again, skirting L around blowdown on the opposite bank.

The hike can be extended beyond this point but the trail is less pleasant and more difficult to follow. Most hikers would end the hike here.

The trail continues to a jct. at 3.4 mi. An unclear path drops off to the R. A compass bearing of due N along this path takes you past an old hunters' open campsite. Just beyond, the way levels but is blocked by water due to beaver activity. Second Pond Flow can be seen through the trees ahead. Maneuvering around to the R will take you past the water and out onto the open meadow of the flow at 3.7 mi. It is many times larger than Bog Meadow, but not as easy to walk. However, it is well worth seeing if you don't mind some discomfort hiking over from Bog Meadow.

The L path from the jct. at 3.4 mi is obvious for about a half-mile, but then becomes extremely difficult to follow. It leads to a clearing at a stream crossing 0.9 mi from the jct. This section should not be attempted except by those with good compass, map-reading, and off-trail hiking experience.

✳ Trail in winter: In winter, with summer growth flattened, this trail is a fine ski route. Just upstream from the bog, there are lovely ponds to explore on skis or snowshoes. The user must be good with maps and take care.

🐾 Distances: To Diamond Brook, 1.3 mi; to Mud Pond Trail, 2.1 mi; to Bog Meadow, 2.5 mi (4.0 km).

(7) Second Pond Trail

Map: C6

The hike to Second Pond makes an extremely nice day trip. It has few grades and passes through magnificent open forests. Second Pond is over half a mile long and is very attractive.

▶ Trailhead: Access is off NY 8, along Chatiemac Rd. This road is 0.5 mi S of Black Mt. Ski Lodge and 1.5 mi N of Bakers Mills. Turn W onto Chatiemac Rd. and gain about 600 ft elevation as you drive 2.3 mi to the trailhead. The unmarked trailhead (0.0 mi) is on the R (N) side of the road, but is easily found. (If you happen to pass the trailhead and reach Chatiemac Club and Chatiemac Lake, turn around and drive 0.3 mi back to the trailhead.) ◀

THE YELLOW-MARKED TRAIL heads generally N. At 0.1 mi a pond can be seen L. Crossing a brook at the pond's dammed outlet, the level route continues onward. At 0.4 mi a meadow is visible far downslope through the trees to the R.

The path climbs very gradually. Its course remains generally N until before Height of Land Mt. to the W. At 0.8 mi the grade increases as the trail ascends a spur. Excellent views of the open woods and large boulders are R of the path. Height of land is attained at 1.1 mi, only 190 ft above the trailhead elevation of 2320 ft.

The trail now swings W until it hugs the steeper sides of Height of Land Mt. A slight loss of elevation occurs at 1.2 mi. The path then stays mostly on contour for the next mile.

At 2.2 mi, the trail begins to descend off the shelf. A gradual swing N and then NE occurs over the next half-mile. A final gradual descent leads to the S shore of Second Pond at 2.7 mi. An open campsite with fire ring is located a short distance back from the shore.

This is an attractive sheet of water about a half-mile in length. An island and hills in the distance draw your interest. The water spreads out in equal expanses both to the R and L. Anglers' paths follow the edge of the shore. Given enough time, a walk around the pond would be enjoyable.

❊ Trail in winter: The grades of this trail are very suitable for intermediate skiers. Some care as to route location is necessary, but the woods are generally so open that navigation is relatively simple, if one's map skills are in good shape.

❧ Distances: To beaver pond, 0.1 mi; to height of land, 1.1 mi; to descent, 2.2 mi; to Second Pond, 2.7 mi (4.4 km).

(7A) **Gore Mt. (Schaefer Trail)**

Maps: Page 48 and B6 (partial)

The trail to the summit of Gore Mt. is named in honor of the Schaefer brothers, Carl, Paul, and Vincent. Paul was a renowned Adirondack conservationist and writer, while Carl and Vincent were major figures in developing skiing on the mountain before the present state-run facility was constructed. The brainchild of Paul's son-in-law, Don Greene, the trail was designed, cut, and marked by Don and other volunteers. It is entirely on public land.

Caution is advised for 200 yd on each side of Daves Cirque and for

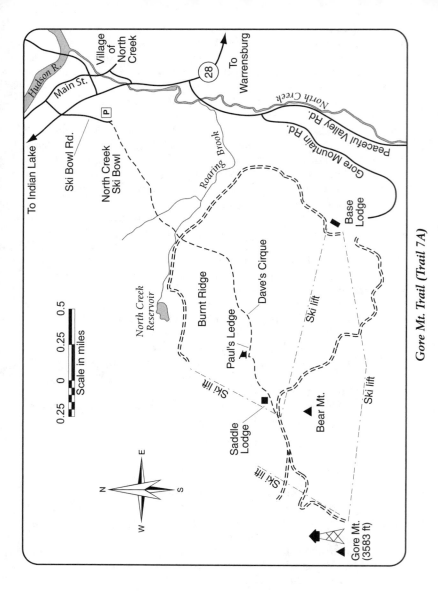

Gore Mt. Trail (Trail 7A)

50 yd beyond Pauls Ledge, since a mountain bike trail overlaps the Schaefer Trail in these locations.

▶ Trailhead: The trailhead is located at the North Creek Ski Bowl. Approaching from the S on NY 28, turn L onto Ski Bowl Road 0.3 mi N of the intersection of NY 28 and NY 28N at North Creek. A large DEC sign for the trail is at the corner, and the North Creek Health Center is on the L. Another DEC sign for the Schaefer Trail is 0.3 mi down the road on the R. Park across from the sign. Maps are available in the trail register, which is on a knoll above the sign. ◀

FROM THE DEC SIGN (0.0 mi), follow blue DEC trail markers SW up the R side of the ski slope. The ski slope levels briefly at 0.2 mi, then continues up steeply to 0.5 mi, where the slope turns R and the trail crosses L and enters the woods.

The trail turns R at an arrow sign at 0.6 mi. It climbs steeply and bears R on a ski trail at 0.7 mi. At 0.8 mi, it reenters the woods at a sign on the L side of the ski trail.

After crossing two streams, the trail continues up a moderate grade until dropping down to cross Roaring Brook at 1.2 mi just above a bridge. The trail immediately crosses a road and begins its climb up to the E shoulder of Burnt Ridge. It reaches a power line at 1.5 mi, with a view of NY 28 downhill to the L. The trail angles L through a raspberry patch to a R turn sign on the opposite side. It follows the power line briefly before turning L into the woods, heading generally S.

The trail ascends steeply to an interesting split boulder (Karate Rock) on the R side of the trail at 1.7 mi. It then continues on a level course until dropping down a moderate slope to a stream at 2.1 mi. The trail was purposely routed here for the hiker's enjoyment. The stream runs through a beautiful open woods glade shaped like an amphitheater (Daves Cirque), with a rock wall defining its upper end.

Less than 100 yd from the stream, the trail passes a pile of rock slabs stacked domino-style against one another (Chanols Rock) on the L. Passing another rock formation on the L, the trail bears R and climbs up a moderate slope. It parallels a rock wall on the R until turning L at 2.4 mi. The trail ascends up a short steep pitch to Pauls Ledge at 2.5 mi. Crane Mt. can be seen to the S, while Gore Mt. is directly ahead (W). Just past Pauls Ledge, 50 ft to the R of the main trail, there is a lean-to.

Leaving the ledge, the trail drops down into a sag, bypasses a swampy area to the L, and continues up a short steep pitch to a ski trail at 2.9 mi. The High Peaks, centered by Mt. Marcy, can be seen to the N from the middle of the slope.

Angling L up the slope, the trail continues into the woods. Immediately before another ski slope, at 3.1 mi the trail turns L. It emerges into the open in 150 yd, turns R up a ski trail, and reaches Saddle Lodge at 3.3 mi.

From the lodge, the trail follows Cloud Trail to the top of the mountain. (A map of the ski trails is on the R just beyond Saddle Lodge.) It continues through the ski lifts on a level course to 3.7 mi, where it turns L and ascends steeply to a R turn at 3.8 mi. From there, it follows the maintenance road as it ascends, often steeply, to the top of Cloud Trail. The trail ends at the fire tower to the R of Cloud Trail at 4.5 mi. The fire tower is closed. However, a variety of views can be found by wandering around the top of the mountain. Particularly notable is the view of the High Peaks from the crest of Cloud Trail.

❋ Trail in winter: Year-round use of the trail is permitted up to Pauls Ledge, but the trail is closed beyond that during the skiing season. Pauls Ledge is a nice destination for a snowshoe climb.

🚶 Distances: To Roaring Brook, 1.2 mi; to power line, 1.5 mi; to Daves Cirque, 2.1 mi; to Pauls Ledge, 2.5 mi; to Saddle Lodge, 3.3 mi; to fire tower, 4.5 mi (7.3 km). Ascent, 2533 ft (772 m). Elevation, 3583 ft (1092 m). ◆

Siamese Ponds
FROM THE EAST

Old Farm Clearing and Thirteenth Lake provide trailhead accesses to the Siamese Ponds Wilderness Area from the NE. The road from North River generally follows the stagecoach route of the 1800s to Old Farm Clearing. From there the stagecoach road to Indian Lake went past Puffer Pond and Kings Flow. Another route went to Bakers Mills. Today, these old roads are hiking trails.

Access is via Thirteenth Lake Rd. off NY 28 at the Hamilton County line just N of North River and S of where the unused (2003) railroad crosses the highway. A DEC sign indicates this is the way to the Siamese Ponds Wilderness Area. Turn S onto Thirteenth Lake Rd. and follow the macadam up the hill.

There is a road jct. at 3.4 mi. The dirt road to the R is Beach Rd. It leads 0.8 mi to the parking area at Thirteenth Lake.

The main road continues across a concrete bridge and leads 0.8 mi to a jct. with a small DEC sign. The R fork (Old Farm Rd.) leads another 0.5 mi to a winter parking area L. A summer parking area is another 0.3 mi ahead, at a trail register and vehicle barricade. Old Farm Clearing is 1.2 mi along a woods road from this point.

Below are some recommended hikes in the area:

SHORT HIKES:
◆ William Blake Pond: 1.6 mi (2.6 km) round trip. A short walk to a pretty pond.
◆ Hooper Mine: 0.8 mi (1.3 km) round trip. A step back into history to look at a garnet mine.
◆ Elizabeth Point: 1.8 mi (2.9 km) round trip. A nice lunch spot on Thirteenth Lake.

MODERATE HIKES:
◆ Peaked Mt. Pond and Peaked Mt.: 7.2 mi (11.6 km) round trip. A day trip to a pretty pond with an option to climb a rocky summit.
◆ Balm of Gilead Mt.: 1.8 mi (2.9 km) round trip. A short climb for a panoramic view of the Siamese Ponds Wilderness Area.

HARDER HIKES:

◆ East Branch Sacandaga Trail: 19.2 mi (31.0 km) round trip. A long trunk trail with several side trips possible.

◆ Puffer Pond: 8.4 mi (13.5 km) round trip. A trip into a large pond with two lean-tos to form a good base camp for more hikes.

TRAIL DESCRIBED	TOTAL MILES (one way)	PAGE
Peaked Mt. Pond and Peaked Mt.	3.6 (5.8 km)	52
William Blake Pond	0.8 (1.3 km)	55
Balm of Gilead Mt.	0.9 (1.5 km)	56
Hooper Mine	0.4 (0.6 km)	56
Old Farm Clearing	1.2 (1.9 km)	57
Elizabeth Point	0.9 (1.5 km)	58
East Branch Sacandaga Trail from Old Farm Clearing	9.6 (15.5 km)	58
East Branch Sacandaga Trail toward Botheration Pond	1.0 (1.6 km)	60
Puffer Pond	4.2 (6.8 km)	61
Hour Pond	1.5 (2.4 km)	62

(8) Peaked Mt. Pond and Peaked Mt. Trail

Map: A5

The trail to Peaked Mt. Pond offers a day hike that is about as perfect as it gets. Seldom does so much variety occur in such a short distance. The pond is lovely, and its setting in the shadow of the bold rocky face of Peaked Mt. provides a photographer's picnic.

▶ Trailhead: The trailhead is at the boat launching area and campsites at the N end of Thirteenth Lake (see page 51). A trail register and trailhead sign are located at the lakeshore. The trail is marked with a combination of red DEC trail markers and circular red blazes. ◀

THE TRAIL HUGS the W edge of Thirteenth Lake. At times it climbs high above the water only to return to the shore again. At a fork at 0.2 mi, a sign points the way to a camping area down the L fork, while the trail bears R up a knoll and around the camping area. A private beach is seen across the lake at 0.5 mi.

When Peaked Mt. Brook enters Thirteenth Lake at 0.8 mi, the trail turns W and follows the N side of the brook upstream. In the next 0.8 mi it gains nearly 300 ft of elevation. However, the grade is so uniformly gradual and the views along the cascading brook so interesting that the ascent seems easy.

At 1.6 mi the trail levels and crosses the brook, soon arriving at the first of three vleis. From here to Peaked Mt. Pond the trail winds around the vleis and crosses the brook several times. The first view of Peaked Mt. is part way around the first vlei.

Beaver activity is evident at all three vleis. The beaver lodge and dam just off the trail on the R at 1.9 mi are hard to miss. Another set is to the L at 2.1 mi. A long curving dam floods a large area just before the brook is crossed for the last time at 2.8 mi.

Climbing a moderate grade, the trail reaches the shore of Peaked Mt. Pond at 2.9 mi. A trail leads L around the S edge of the pond, where a few open campsites are found. A fine view of the mountain is obtained a short distance along this trail.

The trail to this point has been easy and pleasant. Those interested in no more than such a walk may wish to have lunch and enjoy the view of the mountain across the water. The remaining ascent to the summit is far more rugged and very steep in places.

The path around the E end of Peaked Mt. Pond almost immediately crosses the outlet of the pond. The trail parallels the shoreline, though a ways back from the water in most places. At 3.0 mi, the trail reaches the NE corner of the pond, where a narrow cove is found.

The trail skirts the end of the cove and steeply climbs the shoulder of the mountain. At one time, garnet was mined on this part of Peaked Mt. The route often changes direction as it ascends.

At 3.5 mi, the trail breaks out onto open rock for a short distance. Distant peaks and ponds can be seen. Then the path plunges back into the woods for the short remaining distance to the summit at 3.6 mi.

Summit elevation is 2919 ft, 669 ft above the pond. By moving to various open rocky sections of the summit, one can find extremely fine views. Open pit garnet mines can be seen on Ruby Mt. to the NE and on Gore Mt. to the SE. Peaked Mt. Pond is directly below. The mountains of Vermont are farther E. The High Peaks of the Adirondacks unfold to the N. Big, flat-topped Blue Mt. is on the horizon to the NW. Gazing past the flat expanses to the W brings you to Snowy Mt. and the Blue Ridge.

❊ Trail in winter: This is a delightful snowshoe trip in winter, especially in late winter. Crampons are suggested once beyond Peaked Mt. Pond.

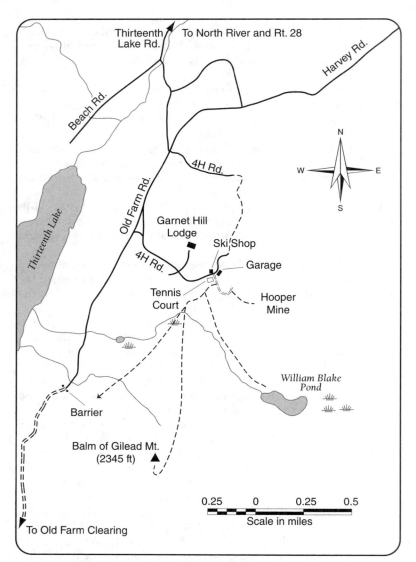

William Blake Pond, Balm of Gilead Mt., and Hooper Mine Trails
(Trails 9, 10, 11)

Distances: To Peaked Mt. Brook, 0.8 mi; to first brook crossing, 1.6 mi; to Peaked Mt. Pond, 2.9 mi; to summit, 3.6 mi (5.8 km). Ascent, 1245 ft (380 m); summit elevation, 2919 ft (890 m).

(9) **William Blake Pond Trail**

Maps: Page 54 and B5

William Blake Pond was originally dammed to provide water for running the Hooper Mine. Today, it is a small pond whose depth varies depending upon the degree of beaver activity. It makes a nice walk and can be combined with the Balm of Gilead climb (trail 10) or the Hooper Mine walk (trail 11) to make a pleasant series of trips that can be completed easily in a single day.

▶ Trailhead: Access is via Thirteenth Lake Rd. off NY 28 at North River, near the Hamilton Co. line road sign. Turn at the DEC signpost marking the route to the Siamese Ponds Wilderness Area.

Follow Thirteenth Lake Rd. SW. At a jct. at 3.4 mi, continue across a concrete bridge. Avoid the R turn onto Beach Rd. Then bear L up the hill at 4.2 mi, avoiding the R fork (Old Farm Rd.) that continues on toward Old Farm Clearing. The L fork has a small sign pointing the way to Garnet Hill Lodge. Continue straight through the jct. at 4.6 mi, instead of going L up the hill to the lodge. A cross-country ski shop is at 4.8 mi from NY 28. Park off the road and follow the supplementary map on page 54. Remember, you are on private land at the courtesy of the Garnet Hill Lodge. ◀

FROM THE L SIDE of the tennis court (0.0 mi), head S on a dirt road a short distance. As the road begins to climb a grade, bear R, where a trail has been brushed out. Almost immediately, bear R again onto the Overlook Trail. This trail winds through the woods, coming to a jct. at 0.2 mi, behind a camp. Turn L at this jct. and follow the unmarked trail S. The E bank of William Blake Pond outlet is soon seen. It is followed 0.6 mi upstream to the pond through a fine deciduous forest. The grade is gradual.

❃ Trail in winter: This trail begins on private land of the Garnet Hill Lodge. A ski ticket should be purchased in winter.

 Distances: To trail jct. near camp, 0.2 mi; to William Blake Pond, 0.8 mi (1.3 km).

(10) Balm of Gilead Mt. Trail

Maps: Page 54 and B5

Balm of Gilead Mt. is a small mountain, but its view is well worth the climb, for it provides an excellent vista into the Siamese Ponds Wilderness Area.

▶ Trailhead: Access is the same as that for the William Blake Pond Trail (trail 9, page 55). Follow the William Blake Pond Trail description to the jct. at 0.2 mi. ◀

FROM THE JCT. at 0.2 mi, continue straight ahead SW. After 200 ft, a well-worn unmarked path bears L (S). The trail is not well maintained, but receives enough use to be easily followed. It climbs gradually through a climax forest. Shortly after crossing a brook at 0.3 mi, it turns L. Red paint blazes mark the way from here.

At 0.5 mi, a red diamond-shaped metal marker is on a large sugar maple. The climbing then becomes moderate.

At 0.9 mi, the trail runs right up to a large boulder and circles L around its base to an open cliff face and fire ring at the summit.

The view is striking. The S end of Thirteenth Lake, with its marshy inlet, dominates the scene. Bullhead Mt. parallels the lake's W shore. Puffer Mt. is to the SW. Bare-topped Peaked Mt. is on the extreme R to the NW. The second bump of Balm of Gilead Mt. is directly to your L front (S) and the shoulder of Eleventh Mt. can be seen in the distance to the L of the bump. A more complete view of Thirteenth Lake can be had by heading N another 100 yd from this spot.

❋ Trail in winter: This is a short but interesting snowshoe trip in winter.

⚎ Distances: To first brook, 0.3 mi; to red metal marker, 0.5 mi; to summit, 0.9 mi (1.5 km). Ascent, 425 ft (130 m). Elevation, 2345 ft (715 m).

(11) Hooper Mine Trail

Map: Page 54 and B5

The Hooper Mine is an abandoned open pit garnet mine on state land. The short walk to it is well worth the effort. The high walls of the open pit and the garnet-rich rock are very unusual.

▶ Trailhead: Access is the same as that for the William Blake Pond Trail (trail 9, page 55). The trail begins at the L side of the tennis court. Follow the dirt road a short distance until it begins to climb a grade.

Bear R onto a path, which after another 50 ft reaches a second jct. Avoid the R turn to the Overlook Trail. Instead, go straight ahead to the SSE. ◄

THE TRAIL PARALLELS the dirt road as it bends around. At 0.2 mi, within sight of a house at the end of the road, the trail to the mine abruptly turns R. It climbs a gradual grade S, but soon makes a large horseshoe bend to the N. The mine is reached at 0.4 mi.

The best view is gained by climbing the rock outcrop to the L of the pit entrance. The bright orange oxidized rock of the pit wall stands out. The pit itself forms a 200 yd diameter amphitheater. The active Ruby Mt. Mine can be seen in the distance to the N.

❄ Trail in winter: This is a very short but worthwhile snowshoe trip. Interesting photography can be had. Since the trail begins on private land of the Garnet Hill Lodge, skiers should purchase a ski ticket.

🐾 Distances: To abrupt R turn, 0.2 mi; to mine, 0.4 mi (0.6 km).

(12) Old Farm Clearing Trail

Map: B5

Only stone foundations amidst the trees provide clues to what the old farm that once occupied this clearing was like. A tree plantation covers most of what must have been open land in the late 1800s.

One used to be able to drive into this spot, where several trailheads are found. After the land was classified as Wilderness, the road eventually was closed to vehicles.

▶ Trailhead: Refer to page 55 for access directions. ◄

THE DIRT ROAD that leads to Old Farm Clearing begins at a stone barrier and trail register at the rear of the summer parking area. From here, rolling grades lead S, high above the E shore of Thirteenth Lake.

Elizabeth Point Trail is on the R at 0.6 mi. The pleasant route through deciduous forest reaches Old Farm Clearing at 1.2 mi. Several trails lead from the far end of the clearing. Informal campsites are found in the trees around the clearing. There is a spring 50 ft S of the clearing.

❄ Trail in winter: Perhaps no short trail is skied as often as this one. Feeder trails from Garnet Hill Lodge to the parking area bring many weekend guests to here and then beyond into the Siamese Ponds Wilderness Area. Because of the relatively high elevation (1800 ft), there is often snow here when none can be found in the lower valleys.

☖ Distances: To Elizabeth Point trailhead, 0.6 mi; to Old Farm Clearing, 1.2 mi (1.9 km).

(13) Elizabeth Point Trail

Map: B5

Elizabeth Point is a small projection of the E shoreline of Thirteenth Lake. It has a picnic table, fireplace, and shallow water tempting the swimmer. It can be reached easily by canoe from the N end of the lake, but makes a very nice walk from the parking area for a picnic.

▶ Trailhead: The trail is unmarked, but easy to find and follow. The trailhead is 0.6 mi along the Old Farm Clearing Trail (trail 12). Here (0.0 mi) the trail gradually descends a narrow footpath W to the shore of Thirteenth Lake, where two informal campsites are found. ◀

AT 0.2 MI, the grade steepens and levels again at 0.3 mi at a campsite, sitting slightly above the water. A short path leads down to a small sandy beach.

The trail continues up a knoll 120 ft to a larger campsite and fireplace. Side trails from this site lead approximately 100 ft to another small sandy beach. Large white pines and birches give way to a view across the lake toward Peaked Mt.

✳ Trail in winter: In deep snow this little trail provides access onto Thirteenth Lake. It requires good control by skiers and may be icy.

☖ Distances: Old Farm Clearing Trail to Elizabeth Point., 0.3 mi (0.5 km); from parking area, 0.9 mi (1.5 km).

(14) East Branch Sacandaga Trail from Old Farm Clearing Trail

Map: B5–D5

This trunk trail is the primary DEC marked trail into the Siamese Ponds Wilderness Area.

▶ Trailhead: Access to the trailhead is from Old Farm Clearing (trail 12, page 57). From the S end of the clearing (0.0 mi), the trail follows blue markers S. The way is over an open woods road through a pine plantation. ◀

THE TRAIL PASSES a spring on the L immediately after the clearing. At 0.1 mi, it reaches a signpost jct. Continue straight ahead. (The R turn is the Puffer Pond Trail [trail 16], see page 61.)

The trail climbs a gentle grade, levels, and at 0.8 mi begins a rolling descent toward the bridge over the East Branch Sacandaga River. The slope is moderate. From 1.0 to 1.4 mi, the trail is badly eroded. At 1.9 mi, the descent slackens and the trail traverses a number of small humps as it approaches and then parallels the East Branch Sacandaga River at L. Rushing water from spillage over a beaver dam can be heard at 2.9 mi. The dam can be seen near the trail at L.

A small grade brings you to the East Branch Sacandaga River at 3.0 mi, some 200 ft lower in elevation than Old Farm Clearing. In 1992 a bridge, suitable for skiing, was built across the East Branch at this point. The now level trail passes through hardwoods. A wide bridge carries it over Cross Brook at 3.9 mi. A large boulder on the L side of the trail is seen at 4.4 mi. It has a brass USGS BM 1677 embedded in its center at eye level.

A large rustic sign on a tree at the R side of the trail marks arrival at Big Shanty Flow at 5.0 mi. It states, "Big Shanty River Driving Camp 1890s."

The route forks R at 5.3 mi. (The L fork is the original trail and is better skiing; however, it bypasses the lean-to.) The trail soon parallels the bank of the East Branch Sacandaga River. The East Branch Sacandaga Trail (trail 4) lean-to and suspension bridge are reached at 5.6 mi. (The trail across the suspension bridge leads 2.3 mi to the Siamese Ponds [trail 5]).

From the lean-to, the trail leaves the stream and rejoins the original trail at 6.1 mi. Burnt Shanty Clearing is passed at 6.9 mi, but only a few old apple trees and a slight widening of the trail indicate the location of this old landmark site. The ford across the East Branch Sacandaga River to the Curtis Clearing Trail is passed at 7.0 mi, though it cannot be seen from the trail. (See Siamese Ponds from the South Section.)

Pleasant trail walking takes you to a clearing at 8.0 mi where Diamond Mt. can be seen to the N at the L side of the trail. Diamond Brook bridge is reached at 8.1 mi. Not long after, the climb over the shoulder of Eleventh Mt. begins; with a gain of almost 300 ft in elevation. The route is uniform in grade. It levels for a short while at 9.2 mi at the col of the ridge. At the end of the col, the trail leaves the old stagecoach road it has been following and, bearing L, drops steeply down to NY 8. (Skiers should be expert to do this last section with speed.) At 9.6 mi, a DEC trail register announces the large NY 8 parking area.

❊ Trail in winter: This trail is an excellent ski trail. Care and control must be exercised from 0.8 mi to the river and from 9.2 mi to the end of the trail. Allow plenty of time for placing vehicles for point-to-point trips.

❧ Distances: To Puffer Pond Trail jct., 0.1 mi; to East Branch Sacandaga River, 3.0 mi; to Cross Brook, 3.9 mi; to Big Shanty Flow, 5.0 mi; to East Branch Sacandaga Trail lean-to, 5.6 mi; to Curtis Clearing Trail jct., 7.0 mi; to Diamond Brook, 8.1 mi; to Eleventh Mt. col, 9.2 mi; to NY 8 trailhead, 9.6 mi (15.5 km).

(15) East Branch Sacandaga Trail toward Botheration Pond

Map: B5

This short trail leads 1.0 mi E from Old Farm Clearing to the East Branch Sacandaga River. It is a pleasant, short walk through the forest in the summer.

▶ Trailhead: Access is from Old Farm Clearing (see page 57). A DEC sign on a tree at the S end of the clearing identifies it as an unmarked trail to the East Branch Sacandaga River. The trail is wide and clear. It heads SE through a conifer plantation and up a gradual grade into deciduous forest. ◀

HEIGHT OF LAND is reached at 0.4 mi. The drop down to the river at 1.0 mi is a bit steeper than the first part of the trip. The woods are open enough to permit travel along the riverbanks.

❊ Trail in winter: This is a very nice trail to the banks of the river. It also provides an easy route to Botheration Pond and The Vly. By skiing up the frozen river, one can have several more miles of cross-country skiing. This should only be done if the ice is thick enough and the skier is careful.

❧ Distances: To height of land, 0.4 mi; to East Branch Sacandaga River, 1.0 mi (1.6 km). 2.2 mi from parking area.

(16) **Puffer Pond Trail**

Puffer Pond Trail is a primary trail leading to the interior of the Siamese Ponds Wilderness. Its branch trails offer many fine alternatives for extended backpacking trips.

▶ Trailhead: Access is off NY 28 in North River. See the section opening (page 51) for directions to the parking lot of the Old Farm Clearing Trail (trail 12). From the rear of the parking area, follow the woods road 1.2 mi to Old Farm Clearing. Pass through the clearing and continue S 0.1 mi on the East Branch Sacandaga Trail from Old Farm Clearing Trail (trail 14) to a jct. This is the Puffer Pond trailhead. The R fork heads for Puffer Pond. (The L fork continues to NY 8 via the East Branch Sacandaga Trail [trail 14]). ◀

FOLLOW BLUE TRAIL MARKERS through a tree plantation. Native growth is soon reached and a long gradual descent begins. The trail is wide. It crosses a major inlet to Thirteenth Lake at 1.0 mi. From this low point of elevation (1700 ft), 484 ft of elevation will be gained to reach Puffer Pond.

A moderate upgrade soon brings you to the sounds of cascading water. Soon, you will see a series of small waterfalls. The trail parallels the R side of Hour Pond Brook, crossing to the L side on a bridge at 1.3 mi. Turning L, the trail on a bridge climbs a small grade to the Hour Pond Trail jct. (trail 17) at 1.5 mi.

Continuing straight ahead, the Puffer Pond Trail crosses Hour Pond Brook again. The trail now gradually ascends rolling terrain. There is a short, wet section at the end of a clearing at 1.9 mi. After paralleling a beaver meadow, the trail turns R and crosses a stream at 2.3 mi. (If coming from the opposite direction, be sure to turn L here. The trail R is a false herd path.)

The gradually rolling terrain eventually becomes almost level. The Twin Ponds footpath jct. is passed, perhaps unnoticed, at 3.6 mi, followed by a short descent to level trail. A somewhat wet section occurs just before Puffer Pond at 4.0 mi.

A side trail L leads 50 yd to a lean-to on the shore of Puffer Pond. Another side trail leads back to the main trail that continues 0.2 mi along the N shoreline to a second lean-to. It sits above the water level at the jct. of the Kings Flow and Puffer Pond Brook Trails (trail 19). Several open campsites are located between the two lean-tos.

✳ Trail in winter: If snow conditions are good, this can be an enjoyable trail; it can be extended via the Puffer Pond Brook Trail to Kings Flow. There is often crusty ice from the 0.1 mi point to 0.3 mi.

🐾 Distances: To Thirteenth Lake inlet, 1.0 mi; to Hour Pond Trail jct., 1.5 mi; to Twin Ponds jct., 3.6 mi; to Puffer Pond jct., 4.2 mi (6.8 km). This is 5.5 mi from the parking area.

(17) Hour Pond Trail

Map: B5

Hour Pond is one of the most attractive of the 67 ponds in the Siamese Ponds Wilderness Area. Its sandy bottom and open shoreline provide a fine setting for a short backpack trip. The trail winds its way over gentle knolls and easy grades. The pond is 3.1 mi from Old Farm Clearing.

▶ Trailhead: The beginning of the trail is where the Puffer Pond Trail (trail 16) crosses Hour Pond Brook for the second time, 1.6 mi from Old Farm Clearing. A DEC sign indicates the trail is unmarked. However, it is in excellent condition and very pleasant to walk. ◀

BRANCHING R from the Puffer Pond Trail (0.0 mi), the route parallels Hour Pond Brook and gradually gains elevation. The brook is heard but seldom seen. At 0.7 mi, the trail drops down briefly to cross a brook.

A large beaver pond floods the trail at 0.8 mi, just after it descends a short moderate grade. This is easily circumvented by crossing the pond outlet on the L side of the pond and then walking across the beaver dam. Turning L (W), the trail skirts a marsh. A second beaver dam is to the L at 1.0 mi.

The trail continues up another gradual grade and circles around to the N. At 1.4 mi, Hour Pond can be seen below to the L through the trees. The trail turns L and at 1.5 mi reaches an open campsite at the pond's edge.

Several open campsites are found along the E shoreline. Bullhead Mt. is across the pond. Hour Pond Mt. is seen in the distance beyond the N end of the very large pond. The view N from the outlet is particularly nice.

🐾 Distances: To first beaver dam, 0.8 mi; to Hour Pond, 1.5 mi (2.4 km). Total distance from the parking area is 4.3 mi.   ◆

Siamese Ponds
FROM THE NORTH

Kings Flow is in the NW corner of the Siamese Ponds Wilderness Area. A dam, constructed to back up water needed for logging in the late 1880s, created the flow.

There are several ways to enter this northern part of the wilderness area. The most commonly used access is across private land at Kings Flow. A small daily parking fee is required. A second access is over IP land from Big Brook Rd. The John Pond trailhead, which avoids private land, is a third entry point.

The Kunjamuk Trail is the major N–S route in this area. It follows the old stagecoach route from Speculator to Indian Lake. The upper end crosses IP land. Use permits are not needed for the IP lands that appear in this section of the guide, but no camping or building of fires is allowed.

Chimney Mt. has unique geological characteristics that have yet to be fully explained. This is a section of the Adirondacks rich in history and woodlore.

The state land W of Kings Flow and E of Indian Lake is excellent hiking and skiing country. It has been underutilized because of the difficulty of access. Some of the trails are unmaintained and receive only sporadic use by hunters and anglers. Nevertheless, this is an area of great beauty. The hiker who is tired of the hordes in more popular areas of the Adirondacks will enjoy the opportunities for solitude here.

Recommended hikes in this section include:

SHORT HIKES:
◆ Chimney Mt.: 2.0 mi (3.2 km) round trip. This truly remarkable geological oddity will draw the curious hiker back to its summit many times.
◆ Clear Pond: 2.2 mi (3.5 km) round trip. A pretty little pond in an attractive setting.

MODERATE HIKES:
◆ John Pond: 4.4 mi (7.1 km) round trip. The cliffs beyond this exquisite pond will beckon the climber.

◆ Puffer Pond: 4.2 mi (6.8 km) round trip. Reaching this pond requires climbing a ridge, but it is worth the effort.

HARDER HIKES:
◆ Kunjamuk Trail: 15.6 mi (25.2 km) round trip. The farther you walk, the more wild it becomes. Over 30.0 mi of routes can be built into a trip down this old road.

TRAIL DESCRIBED	TOTAL MILES (one way)	PAGE
Chimney Mt.	1.0 (1.6 km)	64
Puffer Pond from Kings Flow	2.1 (3.4 km)	66
Puffer Pond Brook	1.9 (3.1 km)	67
Kings Flow East	2.8 (4.5 km)	68
Humphrey Mt.	1.4 (2.3 km)	69
Kunjamuk	7.8 (12.6 km)	70
Round Pond from Kunjamuk	1.5 (2.4 km)	72
Kunjamuk Mt.	1.1 (1.8 km)	73
John Pond	2.2 (3.5 km)	74
John Pond Crossover	3.2 (5.2 km)	76
Clear Pond	1.1 (1.8 km)	77
Center Pond	0.1 (0.2 km)	78

(18) Chimney Mt. Trail

Map: B4

Chimney Mt. is a geologic oddity. Its structure illustrates a complex tectonic origin that has left not only an interesting chimney but also myriad caves around its upper reaches. While fascinating as a short day trip, it may also form the foundation for many years of study for the spelunker and amateur geologist.

▶ Trailhead: Access begins at the intersection of NY 28 and NY 30 in Indian Lake village. Drive S, 0.6 mi on NY 30. Turn L onto Big Brook Rd. After 1.2 mi you will drive over an extensive bridge at Lake Abanakee. Bear R at the fork 2.1 mi past Lake Abanakee. At the crossroads intersection with Hutchins and Moulton Rds., turn R. The Kunjamuk Trail (trail 22) access bridge across Big Brook is on the R at 6.1 mi. Finally, 7.8 mi after leaving NY 30, at Chimney Mt. Wilderness Lodge on Kings Flow there is a specified parking area (1999) with a small daily use fee. Hikers are reminded that this private landowner is permitting access across his property to the Siamese Ponds Wilderness Area as a courtesy to the public. Continuation of this privilege is dependent upon how the public uses it. ◀

WALK E DOWN a dirt road across a mowed field to the DEC trail register at the edge of the woods R (0.0 mi). Bear L from there to another sign indicating the direction of the blue-marked trail up the mountain.

State land begins at 0.2 mi. From there, the route crosses a brook and begins to climb, moderately at first and then steeply. At 0.8 mi, the first of several herd paths heads L. (The herd paths lead to caves and views W of Kings Flow and Round Pond; the higher ones ascend to a ridge opposite the chimney. From there, the chimney can be seen in full profile.)

The trail ascends steeply up a rock massif and breaks out of the trees into the open at 0.9 mi. A small dip in the trail precedes the final rocky ascent to the chimney. Snaking through a narrow rock passage leads to an enclosure of high rocks. To the L it is possible to drop down under huge overhanging rocks to a lookout.

Straight ahead the trail drops briefly. Sidling around to the L of the trail brings you face-to-face with the huge chimney-like formation that gives Chimney Mt. its name. Elevation here is 2500 ft, some 760 ft above the trailhead. The large flat-topped mountain to the N horizon over the chimney's L shoulder is Blue Mt.

The path that descends to the N circles around to the cut between the chimney and the ridge next to it. This is a hazardous route.

The chimney is below the true summit of the mountain, which has an elevation of 2721 ft. The summit can be reached via a 0.2 mi herd path that begins to the R of the trail just before it enters the narrow rock passage to the chimney. The herd path drops into a hollow and heads E on an easy grade. The summit is rocky and provides a 360° panorama. Blue Mt. is N; the High Peaks, NE; Bullhead Mt., E; Puffer Mt., S; Humphrey Mt., SW; and Snowy Mt., W.

❄ Trail in winter: This is a nice snowshoe trail. Steep sections require care.

🐾 Distances: Trailhead to state land, 0.2 mi; to first herd path, 0.8 mi; to clearing, 0.9 mi; to chimney, 1.0 mi (1.6 km). Ascent, 760 ft (232 m). Elevation, 2500 ft (762 m).

(19) **Puffer Pond from Kings Flow Trail**

Map: B4

This is the primary route to Puffer Pond from the N, although two other routes are possible.

▶ Trailhead: Access to the trailhead is the same as that for Chimney Mt. (trail 18). ◀

FOLLOW RED TRAIL MARKERS from the DEC signpost, 0.1 mi E of the Kings Flow parking area. The route heads SE on a wide, grassy road, soon crossing a minor brook on a bridge. At 0.1 mi, the trail leaves the road, forking R at a small sign. (Avoid the L branch, which curves up a grade.) State land begins at 0.3 mi.

Trending E, the route crosses a tributary of Carroll Brook at 0.6 mi. The trail circles the N edge of a beaver meadow and crosses Carroll Brook itself at 0.7 mi. Bullhead Mt. can be seen upstream to the E.

Once across the brook, turn L and follow the trail along the L bank of Carroll Brook. Signs of beaver activity are obvious along the brook. At 1.1 mi the trail leaves Carroll Brook and gradually climbs to higher elevations over a col SE of Bullhead Mt.

The jct. of the John Pond Crossover Trail (trail 24), at 1.3 mi, is surrounded by huge hemlocks at a wide point of the trail. A few trees have indistinct gray paint spots and there are several cut logs. (The blue-marked John Pond Crossover Trail drops down a grade to the N; see trail 24.)

The red-marked Puffer Pond Trail curves R and climbs steadily to height of land in the col, some 460 ft higher than Carroll Brook. After a brief level stretch, the 176 ft descent begins to Puffer Pond. It is moderately steep, except for one minor leveling at 2.0 mi, just after a brook crossing.

One more dip and a slight upgrade lead, at 2.1 mi, to a three-way jct. and a lean-to at Puffer Pond. The lean-to sits on a bank 15 ft above water level. To the L, another 0.2 mi NE along the shoreline trail, is a second lean-to, sitting close to the water off a small side trail. Between the two lean-tos are several informal open campsites.

A blue-marked trail heads NE to Old Farm Clearing and Thirteenth Lake (trail 16; see Siamese Ponds from the East Section). The trail W along Puffer Pond Brook leads to a jct. with the Kings Flow East Trail (trail 21). Puffer Mt. dominates the scene across the pond to the S.

❋ Trail in winter: This is a good snowshoe trail in winter, but the ridge beyond the John Pond Crossover Trail (trail 24) is not suitable for most skiers.

🐾 Distances: To Carroll Brook, 0.7 mi; to John Pond Crossover Trail jct., 1.3 mi; to Puffer Pond, 2.1 mi (3.4 km).

(20) **Puffer Pond Brook Trail**

Map: B4

The Puffer Pond Brook Trail connects Puffer Pond with the Kings Flow East Trail (trail 21). The trail is no longer maintained by DEC, but it is used regularly and is relatively easy to follow. The most enjoyable direction of travel is W from Puffer Pond. (Originally a stagecoach route, its grade is superb for cross-country skiing.)

▶ Trailhead: The trailhead (0.0 mi) begins at the lean-to on the N shore of Puffer Pond where there is a three-way trail jct. (see above). It heads W and then SW, closely following the shoreline of Puffer Pond. Then, at the end of the pond, it swings W away from the water. ◀

AT 0.5 MI, the trail reaches the R bank of Puffer Pond Brook and parallels it for the next mile. As the brook cuts deeper into the valley floor, the trail retains its constant grade. Consequently, the stream is often heard below to the L, but not seen. At other times, cascading waters rush close by the hiker.

The route leaves the brook at 1.5 mi, as the brook's gradient increases. At the first short incline since leaving Puffer Pond, the trail turns N and then NW away from the stream. The way is almost level to 1.7 mi, where the route passes through a narrow gully, cut out by years of wagon use. Here, at a jct., continue straight ahead. (If you turn L, a steep grade leads to Puffer Pond Brook and up again. Eventually, a jct. with Kings Flow East Trail [trail 21] is reached.) Soon after passing a second wagon-worn narrow gully, the trail drops to the jct. with the Kings Flow East Trail (trail 21) at 1.9 mi.

❊ Trail in winter: The gradual grades of an old stagecoach route make this a good winter ski trail, especially for through trips from Old Farm Clearing to Kings Flow.

🐾 Distances: To end of Puffer Pond, 0.4 mi; to Puffer Pond Brook, 0.5 mi; to turn from brook, 1.5 mi; to Kings Flow East Trail jct., 1.9 mi (3.1 km).

(21) **Kings Flow East Trail**

Map: B4–C4

The Kings Flow East Trail heads S along the E shore of Kings Flow. The region it penetrates is less traveled than many sections of the Siamese Ponds Wilderness Area. However, the walk along the flow is generally level and views of the water are extensive.

▶ Trailhead: Access is the same as that for Chimney Mt. (trail 18). From the parking area, head W across the open field to the flagpole in the direction of the water. One hundred yd S of the flagpole, at 150 degrees, cross a small bridge. Continue along the field edge a short distance to a grassy road on the L. This is the beginning of the Kings Flow East Trail (0.0 mi). ◀

THE UNMARKED, wide, grassy lane heads straight S for 0.4 mi to Carroll Brook. Once across the brook the route becomes a path through thick brush. The woods soon open up and Kings Flow is clearly seen at the R of the trail. It remains visible for the next 1.5 mi.

The Puffer Pond Brook Trail (trail 20) branches L at 1.1 mi. The route continues along the flow, becoming a more rolling course. At 1.3 mi, the flow is lost from view. The trail continues S along the base of Puffer Mt., just E of the wet lowlands that drain into Kings Flow.

A brief descent brings the trail to the Puffer Pond Brook crossing at 1.5 mi. An unmaintained spur of the Puffer Pond Brook Trail (trail 20) comes in L. One hundred yd farther on, the trail crosses a smaller stream coming off Puffer Mt.

Several red and silver bottle caps on trees (2003) at the R of the trail at 2.2 mi mark the jct. of the abandoned Wakely Brook Trail to Round Pond. The trail continues S to a second jct. at 2.4 mi. Here, the Humphrey Mt. Trail branches R (see page 69). The East Trail dips slightly and makes a sharp L turn at the jct. It continues S another 0.4 mi before terminating at 2.8 mi. (The USGS topographic map indicates it continues a greater distance, but it is not apparent in the field.)

✳ Trail in winter: This trail is excellent in conjunction with other local trails for cross-country skiing or snowshoeing.

🐾 Distances: To Carroll Brook, 0.4 mi; to Puffer Pond Brook Trail jct., 1.1 mi; to Puffer Pond Brook, 1.5 mi; to Humphrey Mt. Trail, 2.4 mi; to end of trail, 2.8 mi (4.5 km).

Humphrey Mt. Trail (unmaintained)

Map: C4

Humphrey Mt. is the twin-peaked mountain seen to the S as you look down Kings Flow. It makes a nice climb. Most hikers don't bushwhack to the summit. Instead, they try to locate the old garnet mine, which operated during World War I. The trail generally is clear except for some short stretches in its upper reaches. Examine your map well and have your compass ready.

▶ Trailhead: The trailhead (0.0 mi) is located on the R side of the Kings Flow East Trail (trail 21) at the 2.4 mi point (see page 68). There is a little dip in the otherwise level trail just before the jct. The Humphrey Mt. Trail bears R at the jct., while the Kings Flow East Trail makes a L turn. ◀

LEAVING THE TRAILHEAD, the trail follows red plastic disks and, in places, red tape (2003). The trail soon aligns to 230°. At 0.2 mi, the trail drops down a gradual grade. Thick conifers line the trail as it approaches Humphrey Brook at an angle and crosses it at 0.3 mi.

The route winds around a bit before climbing a short steep slope at 0.4 mi. The woods then open up and the trail heads SW. At 0.6 mi, the trail enters a large clearing of brush and downed trees. A lumber camp once stood in this area.

The trail leaves the clearing at 0.8 mi and generally heads S. The grade steepens. The trail turns W at 1.0 mi, now climbing steeply. Then it turns sharply S at 1.1 mi. Markers occasionally are hard to spot as the trail continues its steep ascent.

Curving around to the SW, the trail reaches a conical pile of mine tailings at 1.4 mi. The tailings pile has become overgrown over the years, so much so that it is possible to reach the top before realizing what it is. A narrow, shallow valley leads S from the pile. The mine was a narrow vein and the exact location is difficult to discern, though garnet-bearing rocks from the mining can be spotted.

Hikers planning to continue to the summit must bushwhack from this point.

❋ Trail in winter: This trail is a good winter climb for experienced winter snowshoers.

❄ Distances: To Humphrey Brook, 0.3 mi; to clearing, 0.6 mi; to garnet tailings pile, 1.4 mi (2.3 km). Total from Kings Flow parking area, 3.8 mi (6.2 km). Ascent from trailhead, 720 ft (220 m).

(22) Kunjamuk Trail

The Kunjamuk Trail presents a few challenges that need not deter experienced hikers. Blowdown on Petes Hill slows progress, but needn't stop it. On a through trip, the Kunjamuk River must be waded. In dry weather, this is more fun than challenging. In wet weather, each hiker must make up his or her own mind before trying it. Regardless, those who are looking for an enjoyable walk through wilderness will find that gradual grades and the beauty of the woods amply compensate for any obstacles.

▶ Trailhead: Access is from Indian Lake village via Big Brook Rd. Follow the same access route as for the Chimney Mt. trailhead (see page 64) to the 6.1 mi point. Turn R at the road intersection and cross Big Brook on a wooden bridge. There is a pullout on the R at 0.2 mi, just before the road turns R and ascends a hill. This is the recommended parking area at this time (2003). ◀

THE FIRST 1.6 MI of this route crosses IP land. The hiker is reminded that no IP permit is required to use the trail, but no camping is allowed until state land has been reached.

The trail, marked with blue DEC trail markers, begins on a wide dirt road that heads S into the woods (0.0 mi) as the main road turns R and ascends a hill. (The main road goes to Crotched Pond, but has been privately leased and is no longer open for public use.) A camp is visible L at 0.4 mi. The route changes to a grassy lane at a log collection area at 0.5 mi.

The next approximately three-fourths of a mile often is rutted and muddy from ATV use. At 0.7 mi., a stony road angles R up a hillside. Continue straight. (The road to the R is an alternate route to the T intersection mentioned below.) Avoid woods roads angling L at 0.8 and 0.9 mi. As the trail ascends a moderate grade, two more woods roads angle L at 1.1 mi. Bear R.

The trail then levels as it reaches a T intersection at 1.2 mi. A camp is on the R. Turn L and avoid all side roads. As the main route curves R at 1.3 mi, the Kunjamuk Trail–Round Pond Connector Trail (see page 72) cuts back to the L.

Care must be taken at 1.4 mi, where the trail makes a L turn off the grassy road into the woods. ATVs have churned up the trail and made a loop around a mud hole a short distance into the woods (2000).

Continue straight through the loop.

At 1.6 mi, avoid climbing a moderate grade. (This leads to a timber collection area and large turnabout.) Instead, turn L onto a narrower, level woods road. State land and a barrier cable are found 150 ft along this road. The contrast between lumbered land and wilderness land is great. The way is shaded and is far more enjoyable to walk. The grassy trail winds around from S to SW.

Round Lake is soon seen through the trees, just before a trail jct. at 2.1 mi. An open campsite and path to the lake are L. The R turn leads 0.2 mi to a private camp. The Kunjamuk Trail continues straight ahead, staying in sight of the lake. Magnificent white birches line the shore. The trail gains slight elevation and the higher contour provides excellent viewing of the water. As many as four beaver houses can be seen at one time. The trail is excellent.

The trail crosses a creek at 2.8 mi near the end of the lake. It makes a sharp L turn with a camp in view and ascends a minor grade at 3.2 mi. The unmarked Kunjamuk Mt. Trail (see page 73) begins on the R at a trail jct. at 3.8 mi, just after a creek crossing. The trail narrows somewhat, but is easy to follow. At 4.1 mi, a large bog meadow is visible L and the trail crosses another creek at 4.4 mi.

At 5.2 mi, spruces close in on the trail, which crosses a very minor, wet mossy spot at 5.3 mi. The route opens up again and crosses Wakely Brook on an old beaver dam. The source of Wakely Brook is the marsh upstream.

Now the long gradual climb over the E shoulder of Petes Hill begins. Tape markers on trees are very common from this point to the Kunjamuk River. Petes Hill was severely affected by a microburst storm in 1995, and blowdown is frequently encountered on this section of the trail. However, with a bit of persistence and careful attention to the red tape markers, the route can be followed without much difficulty. Height of land at 6.2 mi is hardly noticed. Elevation loss is gradual at first as Petes Hill is descended, but increases more rapidly toward the bottom.

A stream can be heard at 7.6 mi and soon East Brook comes into view 50 ft L through the trees. The wide but shallow brook angles its way through tilted rock joints. The trail makes a sharp R turn and at 7.7 mi reaches a very wide, open meadow. In summer, this meadow is a waist-deep sea of grass. Follow the L edge straight across the meadow for 0.1 mi to the small beginning of the Kunjamuk River at 7.8 mi.

It drains both Rock and Long ponds. In dry weather, wading this river is easy if you don't stand still too long and sink into the muddy bottom. (For continuation of this trail S, refer to the Cisco Creek Trail [trail 38] in the Kunjamuk section of this book.)

❀ Trail in winter: This trail is not suitable as a point-to-point for skiers because of the blowdown on Petes Hill. However, a round trip on the N section would be very pleasant.

♞ Distances: To state land, 1.6 mi; to Round Lake, 2.1 mi; to S end of Round Lake, 2.8 mi; to Kunjamuk Mt. Trail jct., 3.8 mi; to Wakely Brook, 5.6 mi; to height of land, 6.2 mi; to East Brook, 7.6 mi; to Kunjamuk River, 7.8 mi (12.6 km).

Round Pond from Kunjamuk Trail (unmaintained)

Map: B4

This trail provides an easy route to the E side of Round Pond and an attractive vista.

▶ Trailhead: The trailhead is found 1.3 mi along the Kunjamuk Trail (trail 22) from Big Brook Rd. After climbing a curving grade and passing a cabin at R, the trail reaches a T intersection at 1.2 mi and turns L. Another road fork is reached after 0.1 mi, as the main route curves R to the W. The trail to Round Pond is the unmarked, wide, grassy woods road that cuts sharply back L on this curve. ◀

FROM THE TRAIL JCT. (0.0 mi), follow the woods road E, bearing 100°. The trail is flat and clear to a jct. at 0.3 mi. The trail to Round Pond turns R and heads S. (The woods road continues E across posted land to the dam at Kings Flow. The owner's permission is needed to cross it.)

The path reaches another jct. at 0.7 mi. (The path back to the L crosses the posted land mentioned above.) Bear R. After crossing the outlet of Round Pond at 1.4 mi, the trail reaches an open campsite and fire ring on the E shore of the pond at 1.5 mi.

Crotched Pond Mt. lies due W across the pond and the more peaked Kunjamuk Mt. is to the SW. The old Kunjamuk Trail passes along the opposite shore, well out of sight. (The trail continuing S is the old Wakely Brook Trail. It has been abandoned and should not be attempted.)

❀ Trail in winter: For cross-country skiers with good route-finding skills, this trail offers a nice outing. The return trip can be varied by crossing the pond and skiing back to Big Brook Rd. on the Kunjamuk

Trail (trail 22).

🚶 Distances: To trailhead from Big Brook Rd., 1.3 mi. To first jct. from trailhead, 0.3 mi; to second jct., 0.7 mi; to Round Pond shore, 1.5 mi (2.4 km).

Kunjamuk Mt. Trail (unmaintained)

Map: B3–C3

The Kunjamuk Mt. Trail is what remains of the old road that led off the Kunjamuk Trail around the E side of Crotched Pond, to join the N road from Big Brook Rd.

▶ Trailhead: The trail begins at a jct. on the W side of the Kunjamuk Trail (trail 21) 3.8 mi S of the Big Brook trailhead and 1.0 mi from the S end of Round Lake. It heads W as a good woods road up a long, gradual grade and then swings N. ◀

A GRADUAL DESCENT at 0.2 mi leads to a low spot, flooded by beaver. This is easily bypassed on the L at 0.4 mi. Gradual climbing leads to a second beaver flow, which again is easily passed on the L. More climbing leads to an open meadow at 0.6 mi where the remains of an old lumber camp can be seen.

Moderate grades head NW to height of land at 0.9 mi. This is an ideal place to begin a bushwhack up Kunjamuk Mt. Height of land is at 2180 ft. Another 769 ft of ascent up the N side of the mountain takes you to the 2949 ft (899 m) summit.

The old road can be followed for another 0.2 mi. It rapidly dissipates to a confusing bushwhack.

❄ Trail in winter: Too far in the woods for day trips, this mountain could make a winter climb for overnight campers.

🚶 Distances: To open meadow, 0.6 mi; to height of land, 0.9 mi; to terminus of clear trail, 1.1 mi (1.8 km). Total distance from trailhead, 4.9 mi (7.9 km).

(23) John Pond Trail

Map: Page 75 and A4

John Pond is a beautiful sheet of water with a lean-to providing views of handsome cliffs in the distance across the pond. The route still retains some of the ruts dug out prior to the closing of the woods road to motorized vehicles. However, the forest en route makes for an attractive trip. A bushwhack to Clear Pond over the ridge across the lake from the lean-to makes a nice loop trip.

▶ Trailhead: Access is from the intersection of NY 30 and NY 28 in the village of Indian Lake. Head 0.6 mi S on NY 30. Turn L onto Big Brook Rd. and drive 3.3 mi to Starbuck Rd. Turn L and follow Starbuck Rd. 0.4 mi to the entrance of the Wilderness Lodge. Immediately past the entrance, take the L fork, which is Lake View Dr. Go 0.5 mi to a T intersection. Turn R and drive 0.2 mi to its end. From the snowplow turnaround at the end, drive 0.1 mi S on a single-lane woods road to the trailhead parking lot. There is room for four or five vehicles. ◀

FROM THE TRAIL REGISTER (0.0 mi), blue markers lead S along the woods road. The level route continues to a fork at 0.6 mi, where the route makes a sharp turn L to the E. (Informal campsites are found straight ahead, a short distance in the woods by a stream.)

The trail continues SE on nearly level ground, generally paralleling John Pond Brook. At 1.2 mi, the forest opens on the R. Bullhead Mt. to the SE overlooks John Pond Brook flowing through a meadow.

The route turns NE, just as it crosses the Hamilton County line into Warren County, at 1.3 mi. A side trail L, at 1.6 mi, leads up a small grade to the grave sites of Peter Savary and Eliza Emilia King, children who died of diphtheria in 1897.

At 1.7 mi, the trail crosses the outlet to John Pond. The John Pond Crossover Trail (trail 24) to the Puffer Pond Trail from Kings Flow (trail 19) enters from the R at 1.8 mi. A good open campsite is found just across a brook, 0.2 mi along this side trail.

The terrain becomes rolling as elevation increases in the last 0.4 mi to John Pond. A side path to the L at 2.1 mi leads 100 ft to a fish barrier dam.

The lean-to at John Pond is at 2.2 mi. Beaver have dammed the pond outlet, deepening this 0.3 mi long pond. The cliffs across the water rise nearly 500 ft, forming an open rock ridge from which views of the High Peaks can be found.

(The easiest way to reach the ridge is to return 0.1 mi back to the fish barrier dam. Cross the outlet at the dam base, bushwhack W up to the ridge, and walk it N. Hikers who are proficient with a map and compass may wish to extend the bushwhack to Clear Pond. Continue N along the ridge, then descend through open woods until intersecting

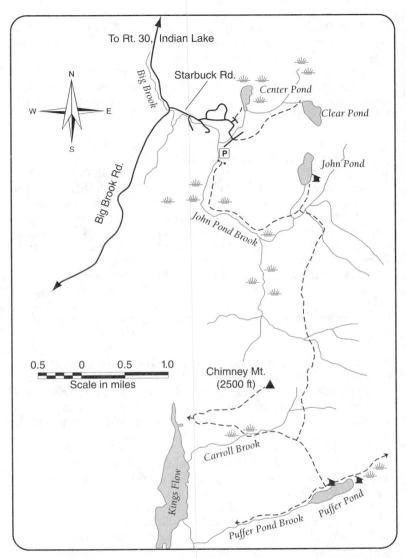

John Pond, John Pond Crossover, Clear Pond, and Center Pond Trails
(Trails 23, 24, 25, 26)

the Clear Pond Trail. To complete a loop to the John Pond trailhead, continue to the Clear Pond trailhead at the T intersection, turn L, and L again at the snowplow turnaround.)

❄ Trail in winter: This trail is an excellent ski route in winter.

🐾 Distances: To E turn in trail, 0.6 mi; to county line, 1.3 mi; to burial site side trail, 1.6 mi; to John Pond Crossover Trail jct., 1.8 mi; to John Pond, 2.2 mi (3.5 km).

(24) John Pond Crossover Trail

Maps: Page 75, A4–B4

This trail connects the John Pond Trail (trail 23) with the Kings Flow to Puffer Pond Trail (trail 19), providing the hiker with several options for extending or varying backpacking trips. It is an excellent wilderness trail, perhaps better reflecting what many believe to be the true essence of wilderness than do some of the older, more developed trails. It has gentle, long grades and crosses several brooks.

▶ Trailhead: The trail begins at the 1.3 mi point on the Kings Flow to Puffer Pond Trail (trail 19). From the jct. (0.0 mi), follow blue trail markers N. The route tends to be wet from 0.2 to 0.4 mi, but this is not a problem except in wet weather. Conditions for the rest of the route are good. ◀

AT **1.5** MI a rock shelf resides on the L for 100 yd. Just past this point the trail swings slightly L and begins a long descent. From 2.0 to 2.1 mi thick undergrowth and occasional blowdowns require care. After crossing a brook at 2.2 mi, the trail levels and opens up considerably.

At a jct. at 2.7 mi, turn W and head downslope. (The path straight ahead continues N for about a mile before terminating.)

The trail enters a tree plantation at 2.9 mi, crossing a brook twice and then a meadow. The trail then becomes a grassy road. The jct. with the John Pond Trail (trail 23) is at 3.2 mi. John Pond is 0.4 mi N along the John Pond Trail.

❄ Trail in winter: This trail can be used to join the Puffer Pond to Kings Flow Trail (trail 19) to the John Pond Trail (trail 23). This is a true backwoods trip, requiring adequate skills and forest knowledge.

🐾 Distances: Puffer Pond Trail to rock shelf, 1.5 mi; to jct., 2.7 mi; to John Pond Trail, 3.2 mi (5.2 km). Total distance from Kings Flow to John Pond, 4.9 mi (7.9 km).

(25) Clear Pond Trail

Maps: Page 75 and A4

The trail to Clear Pond makes a nice short walk to a pretty body of water. The route passes through mature deciduous forest. The trip can be extended by a short bushwhack over the ridge to the John Pond Trail (trail 23).

▶ Trailhead: To reach the trailhead, follow the same access directions as for the John Pond trail (see page 74) to the T intersection. The trailhead has been relocated from its prior position up the road L. It now is located on the S side of the road at the T intersection. Although it may be a bit difficult to see in the foliage, a DEC sign on a tree identifies the trail. ◀

AFTER CLIMBING the road bank, the trail follows red markers SE up a gradual grade. At 0.1 mi, it turns R, still heading SE. At 0.2 mi, it turns E, beginning a 0.3 mi curve around to the NE. The old trail enters sharply from the L (W) at 0.5 mi. (Remember to turn L at this jct. on the return trip.) Bearing R, the trail stays on contour to 0.6 mi, where it ascends a moderate slope to 0.8 mi and then levels.

At 0.9 mi, the trail begins a moderate descent to the pond. It crosses the pond outlet L at 1.0 mi, follows the shore of the pond, and ends at an informal campsite on the N shore at 1.1 mi. The shoreline has been enlarged by beaver activity. Consequently, the informal paths around the pond have been flooded in places, especially on the S side.

❋ Trail in winter: This is an intermediate backwoods trail with possible skiing on Clear Pond if conditions permit. Locating the trailhead may be difficult in winter.

🐾 Distances: To trail jct., 0.5 mi; to pond outlet, 1.0 mi; to Clear Pond, 1.1 mi (1.8 km).

(26) Center Pond Trail

Maps: Page 75 and A4

Center Pond is a small, marsh-edged body of water. The very short walk to its shore takes only a few minutes.

▶ Trailhead: Follow the trail access directions for the John Pond trailhead (page 74) to the fork in the road at the entrance of the Wilderness Lodge. Take the L fork, which is Lake View Drive. Turn onto the third side road to the L, 0.3 mi along Lake View Drive. (If you miss it, turn around at the T intersection and drive back 0.2 mi to the side road.) A gray house is kitty-corner to the side road.

Although it might appear to be a driveway for a house on its R, the side road continues past the house, turns L, and dead-ends at a brown building. A small grassy turnout is on the R, 0.1 mi along the road, within sight of the brown building. ◄

AN UNMARKED PATH leads N from this grassy turnout to the pond. The path is a little over 0.1 mi long. It ends at the marshy shore of the pond near a large rock one can stand on to view the water. A short channel extends out to the deeper part of the pond; water lilies blanket its S end.

❋ Trail in winter: This is a very short trail but would be suitable for snowshoeing.

🚶 Distances: To Center Pond, 0.1 mi (0.2 km).   ◆

In the chimney of Chimney Mountain
ROB MEYER

Indian Lake Section

When the Penobscot Indian Sabael Benedict discovered Indian Lake during the Revolutionary War period, it was actually a series of three small lakes. The mouth of Squaw Brook is the burial place of his wife, and nearby Snowy Mt. was then called Squaw Bonnet Mt.

Lumber interests first built a dam at the foot of Indian Lake in 1845, building a larger second dam in the 1860s. This deepened the waters some 33 ft and created the present lake.

The S end of Indian Lake, almost all of the E shoreline, and all of the lake's islands are state land. Distributed at intervals along the shore and on islands are 55 designated campsites. Each has a fireplace, table, and privy. Six open picnic sites at various locations around the lake are also available for day use. Public access to the lake is from the state boat launch near the Lewey Lake Public Campground and from a few privately owned marinas at Sabael.

In season, all campsites must be reserved. This can be done at the Indian Lake Islands Campground headquarters, across the road from Lewey Lake Public Campground on NY 30. Each site is numbered. A free map locating them is available at the headquarters. A charge for each night of camping is levied.

Almost unbounded opportunities for hiking and canoeing are available. The state land to the E of Indian Lake is true wilderness. Trails lead to John Mack Pond and other parts of the Siamese Ponds Wilderness Area. Snowy Mt. and Baldface Mt. have DEC trails. The Sucker Brook Trail leads into the West Canada Lakes Wilderness Area. Cellar Mt. and Lewey Mt. are reasonable bushwhacks from the Sucker Brook Trail. The 14 miles of Indian Lake, Lewey Lake, and the Jessup River offer significant opportunities for paddling.

Also included in this section are trails off the Cedar River Rd., Wakely Mt., Wakely Dam, and an introduction to the Moose River Recreation Area.

Following are recommended hikes in the Indian Lake area:

SHORT HIKES:

◆ Sprague Pond: 0.8 mi (1.3 km) round trip. An easy walk to a pretty pond.
◆ Baldface Mt.: 2.2 mi (3.5 km) round trip. Seldom has such a magnificent view been gained from such a short climb.

MODERATE HIKES:

◆ John Mack Pond: 3.2 mi (5.2 km) round trip. A nice woods walk to a lovely pond.
◆ Wakely Mt.: 6.0 mi (9.7 km) round trip. The first part is easy, but once climbing begins, it's very steep.

HARDER HIKES:

◆ Snowy Mt.: 7.8 mi (12.6 km) round trip. Almost a 4000 ft peak, this is a challenging trip.
◆ Sucker Brook Trail: 15.4 mi (24.8 km) round trip. This connector trail to the Northville-Placid Trail is a real wilderness hike.

TRAIL DESCRIBED	TOTAL MILES (one way)	PAGE
Bullhead Pond	0.6 (1.0 km)	81
Whortleberry Pond	3.1 (5.0 km)	81
Big Bad Luck Pond	0.7 (1.1 km)	83
Ross Pond	0.3 (0.5 km)	84
Dug Mt. Brook Falls	0.4 (0.6 km)	86
Sucker Brook	7.7 (12.4 km)	86
Watch Hill from NY 30	1.2 (1.9 km)	88
Watch Hill from Indian Lake	0.5 (0.8 km)	89
Snowy Mt.	3.9 (6.3 km)	90
John Mack Pond	1.6 (2.6 km)	91
John Mack Pond–Long Pond Cross	2.2 (3.5 km)	92
Crotched Pond	1.5 (2.4 km)	93
Baldface Mt.	1.1 (1.8 km)	94
Sprague Pond	0.4 (0.6 km)	95
Stephens Pond from McCanes	2.5 (4.0 km)	95
Wakely Mt.	3.0 (4.8 km)	97
Moose River Recreation Area	0.0 (0.0 km)	98

(26A) **Bullhead Pond Trail**

Map: Page 82

From a contemporary perspective, the name of this pond is curious. However it was first named, DEC began stocking the pond with trout in 1951, and now it is prized more for its trout than its bullheads. The trail is more likely to be used by anglers than hikers. Nevertheless, it offers an easy and pleasant walk to a nice pond.

▶ Trailhead: Access is off Chain Lakes Rd. near Indian Lake. Chain Lakes Rd. leaves NY 28 1.3 mi E of the Rt. 28/30 intersection in Indian Lake. Traveling W on NY 28, Chain Lakes Rd. is on the R immediately past Lake Abanakee. Head N on Chain Lakes Rd. to a large parking lot on the L at 1.4 mi (0.3 mi beyond the Lake Abanakee dam). The trailhead is at the back of the parking lot. ◀

CLIMBING THE BANK of the parking lot, the red-marked trail continues up a moderate slope and levels after 100 yd. Heading NNW, it follows an old woods road through a pine forest. The grades are easy. At a jct. at 0.5 mi, the trail continues straight ahead and the woods road turns R. Shortly thereafter, the trail drops down a moderate slope, bears R, and reaches the S shore of the pond at 0.6 mi. DEC signs detailing fishing restrictions are prominent.

❄ Trail in winter: This trail would be suitable for a short snowshoe trip.

🦶 Distances: To jct., 0.5 mi; to pond, 0.6 mi (1.0 km).

(26B) **Whortleberry Pond Trail**

Map: Page 85

Whortleberry Pond is the northernmost of three ponds sharing the same trailhead on NY 28, the others being Ross and Big Bad Luck Ponds. The three ponds are close enough to be visited in one day.

▶ Trailhead: Access is off the N side of NY 28, 7.2 mi E of the NY 28/30 intersection in Indian Lake and 4.9 mi W of the Thirteenth Lake Rd./NY 28 intersection in North River. A macadam parking lot for the trailhead is 0.2 mi farther E on the S side of NY 28. Large DEC signs identify the trailhead and parking lot. ◀

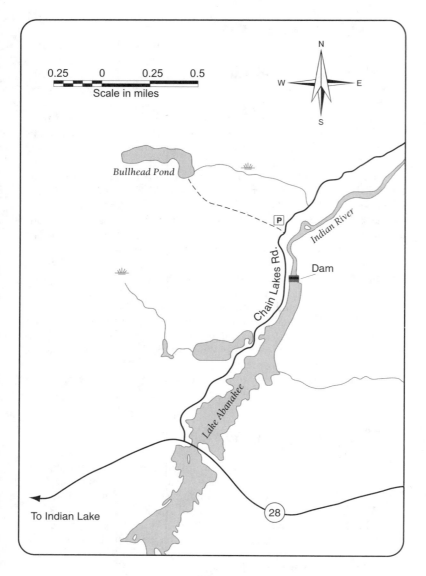

Bullhead Pond Trail (Trail 26A)

THE RED-MARKED TRAIL drops down a steep road bank to a DEC trail register (0.0 mi). Heading N, the trail immediately passes through a short muddy stretch. At 0.1 mi, it turns R at a trail sign and crosses a small stream on two hewn logs.

After a few minor ups and downs, at 0.4 mi the trail bears R up a moderate grade and swings around to the NE. Topping at 0.5 mi, it then begins a long gradual descent to Bell Mt. Brook, which it crosses on several logs thrown across the stream at 1.1 mi.

From the brook, the trail heads up a moderate grade and swings around to the W. It reaches a col on the NE shoulder of Bell Mt. at 1.6 mi, having gained 260 ft. Several rock faces are on the R as the trail passes through the col.

Although several knolls are encountered along the way, the trail gradually loses elevation in the next mile-plus. The first sighting of a marsh on the R is at 1.8 mi. The trail levels briefly at 1.9 mi as it passes the marsh R and blowdown L. At 2.0 mi, just before more blowdown, it turns N. After a few more ups and downs, the trail heads up a small knoll to the jct. with the yellow-marked Ross Pond Trail (trail 26D) at 2.3 mi. Continue straight.

Passing over several more small humps, at 2.7 mi the trail reaches the jct. with the blue-marked Big Bad Luck Pond Trail (trail 26C). Continuing straight, the Whortleberry Pond Trail gradually descends to 2.8 mi, where it makes a brief turn W to another jct. Turning R (N) here, the trail levels. (The trail L is a 0.1 mi shortcut to the Big Bad Luck Pond Trail. Marked with red tape, it heads SW through a glen before climbing a moderate grade to a point 0.1 mi along the Big Bad Luck Pond Trail.)

The trail crosses a rocky clearing at 3.0 mi before dropping down a short, moderate stretch to the tree-lined S shore of Whortleberry Pond at 3.1 mi.

❋ Trail in winter: This trail is suitable for intermediate skiers or snowshoers.

⚶ Distances: To height of land, 0.5 mi; to Bell Mt. Brook, 1.1 mi; to col, 1.6 mi; to Ross Pond Trail jct., 2.3 mi; to Big Bad Luck Pond jct., 2.7 mi; to jct. with shortcut, 2.8 mi; to Whortleberry Pond, 3.1 mi (5.0 km).

26C Big Bad Luck Pond

Map: Page 85

Bad fishing? Bad hunting? An accident? Without knowing what led to the naming of the pond, the mind conjures up all kinds of possibilities on the trail to Big Bad Luck Pond.

▶ Trailhead: The blue-marked trail begins at a jct. 2.7 mi along the Whortleberry Pond Trail (trail 26B). ◀

FROM THE WHORTLEBERRY POND TRAIL, the trail to Big Bad Luck Pond heads W up over a small knoll. Once over the knoll, the trail is level to the pond. Much of the way is through a pine forest. The trail comes to a jct. at 0.1 mi. Continue straight. (The trail marked with red tape to the R is a shortcut to the Whortleberry Pond Trail [trail 26B].) At 0.4 mi, it crosses a small inlet stream. The pond can be seen R. The trail reaches the shoreline at 0.5 mi and turns L (S) briefly then W as it follows the S shore of the pond.

The trail ends at a small cove on the narrow eastern arm of the pond at 0.7 mi. Although there is a view W along the pond, fuller views can be had by bushwhacking farther W along the shoreline.

❋ Trail in winter: Although this trail is level, when skiing, consideration must be given to the grades on the Whortleberry Pond Trail.

❊ Distances: To shortcut jct., 0.1 mi; to stream, 0.4 mi; to shoreline, 0.5 mi; to cove, 0.7 mi (1.1 km). Total distance from NY 28, 3.4 mi (5.5 km).

(26D) Ross Pond Trail

Map: Page 85

The attractiveness of Ross Pond is enhanced by two small islands and a rocky shelf at the shore that invites a swim.

▶ Trailhead: The yellow-marked trail begins at a jct. 2.3 mi along the Whortleberry Pond Trail (trail 26B). Ross Pond can be glimpsed through the trees from the jct. ◀

HEADING E on a gentle downgrade, the trail soon drops down a short, moderate pitch, turns R, and contours a knoll on the S shore of the pond. Dropping down another short, moderate slope, at 0.1 mi it crosses an inlet stream. Climbing up a moderate grade from the stream, the trail then gradually ascends as it skirts the shoreline.

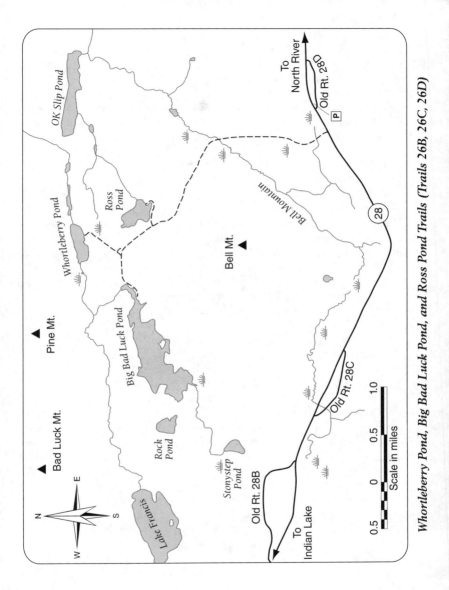

Whortleberry Pond, Big Bad Luck Pond, and Ross Pond Trails (Trails 26B, 26C, 26D)

At 0.2 mi, the trail drops down to the SE corner of the pond, turns L, and crosses a brook. It then climbs R up a small bluff to a camping area at 0.3 mi. From the camping area, a path leads down to a rocky shelf at the shoreline. One of the two islands is directly ahead.

❋ Trail in winter: The pond is a nice destination for a winter outing, but the trail from the junction is more suitable for snowshoeing than skiing.

🐾 Distances: To inlet stream, 0.1 mi; to SE corner, 0.2 mi; to camping area, 0.3 mi (0.5 km). Total distance from NY 28, 2.6 mi (4.2 km).

(27) Dug Mt. Brook Falls Trail

Map: D2

There is a pretty little waterfall at the mouth of Dug Mt. Brook, where it enters the Jessup River. Beside it is a picnic area with a fireplace. While this is an attractive spot for lunch after a paddle up the Jessup from Indian Lake, many people don't realize a much higher waterfall is upstream.

▶ Trailhead: Access is via watercraft on the Jessup River. The boat access at the Indian Lake Islands Campground headquarters near Lewey Lake is one good put-in point. ◀

FROM THE PICNIC AREA (0.0 mi), follow the unmarked path upstream along the N bank of Dug Mt. Brook. The path soon leads to higher ground a short distance back from the waterway. At 0.2 mi it again nears the brook at a point where it bends sharply to the S.

The trail drops down a grade to the water's edge, crosses a small tributary, and climbs to the top of a low, elongated ridge covered with small spruce. Below, the sounds of rapidly moving water may be heard. At 0.4 mi, the path descends to a pool at the base of a 40 ft high waterfall. The trail then ascends to the top of the cataract, where it terminates.

❋ Trail in winter: This is a destination only the adventurous would select in winter. The Panther Pond–Jessup River Trail and an ice crossing could be an access route if the ice were thick enough. Much caution is required whenever on ice.

🐾 Distances: To S brook bend, 0.2 mi; to Dug Mt. Falls, 0.4 mi (0.6 km).

(28) Sucker Brook Trail

Map: C1–C2

The Sucker Brook Trail is a connector trail to the Northville-Placid (N-P) Trail (trail 37). It is not heavily used because considerable climbing is required to reach the col between Lewey and Cellar Mts. However, it is a true wilderness trail with much to offer the hiker, especially the backpacker on a weekend trip.

▶ Trailhead: The trailhead is reached off the W side of NY 30, N of Lewey Lake. Just N of the bridge over the Lewey Lake outlet, a macadam road heads W into the state campground. A sign marks the trailhead a short distance down the road on the R. Please do not obstruct the campground road. Parking is available at a large pullout on the L, 0.3 mi N of the Lewey Lake outlet bridge. ◀

THE TRAIL HEADS W through a hardwood forest. Wide and well-marked with red DEC trail markers, it climbs very gradually. It turns R on a woods road at 0.4 mi and then, within a few yards, L off the road at a DEC trail register. Sucker Brook can be heard, but not seen, to the L. A large tributary stream is crossed at 1.5 mi.

A steady grade proceeds upward to 2.7 mi, where the grade levels. Then, at 3.1 mi the route markedly steepens to the col between Lewey and Cellar Mts. at 3.5 mi and an elevation of 2870 ft (1210 ft higher than the trailhead). (This col is often used as the jump-off point for the relatively easy, open-woods bushwhack up Lewey Mt. and for the more difficult bushwhack through blowdown up Cellar Mt.) The col is level and has ferns and red spruce.

As the trail begins its descent beyond the col, a significant difference is evident. The trail is now much more a path. However, it is easy to follow and is well marked. It is a real wilderness trail from this point forward.

The trail crosses Colvin Brook, reached at 4.4 mi, 10 times before diverging from it. The trail passes through a swampy area shortly after the tenth crossing, but the remainder of the way to the lean-to is level and dry.

The trail reaches the lean-to beside Cedar River at 6.6 mi. The river can usually be rock-hopped, although it is quite wide. The trail heads NW another 1.1 mi, intersecting the N-P Trail (trail 37) at 7.7 mi. (From this point, it is 3.5 mi S over Lamphere Ridge to the dam at First Cedar Lake and 6.0 mi N to Wakely Dam.)

❋ Trail in winter: The trail up to the col is a good access route for winter bushwhack trips of Cellar and Lewey Mts. Beyond the col is not recommended for winter use.

❀ Distances: To tributary crossing, 1.5 mi; to col, 3.5 mi; to Colvin Brook, 4.4 mi; to lean-to on Cedar River, 6.6 mi; to N-P Trail, 7.7 mi (12.4 km). Ascent to col, 1210 ft (369 m).

(29) Watch Hill from NY 30 Trail

Map: B2

Watch Hill is a small mountain that makes an excellent beginner's climb. It offers a variety of trail conditions, ending with a magnificent view of Snowy Mt. and the S end of Indian Lake.

▶ Trailhead: Access to the trailhead is off the E side of NY 30, 1.1 mi S of the Snowy Mt. parking area. This is 8.0 mi S of the NY 28/30 intersection at Indian Lake and 3.4 mi N of the Lewey Lake outlet bridge. The unmarked trailhead is a well-defined, grassy woods road that angles into the forest. Care must be taken in locating the trailhead. ◀

FROM THE TRAILHEAD (0.0 mi), the open woods road heads E, crossing Griffin Brook near the remains of an old log bridge at 0.1 mi. The route becomes more of a path for a short way, as it climbs a small grade. A level section leads to another grade. Near height of land, at 0.7 mi, an orange-painted metal stake is driven into the ground and a trail sign points the way up the hill; the route leaves the woods road to the R (SE) here. It is not marked, but is easy to follow. Avoid a side trail L at 0.8 m. (This alternate 0.4 mi route rejoins the hiking trail farther up the mountain. Horseback riders use it in the summer because of its easy grades. It is the recommended snowshoe route in winter.)

Continuing straight ahead, the hiking trail abruptly becomes steep and angles up the W side of Watch Hill. The trail soon levels. After a few more ups and downs, it reaches a T intersection at 0.9 mi, where the alternate route rejoins the trail from the L. (Note this spot; it is easy to walk past it on the return trip.)

The route turns R at this intersection and heads SW. Soon, it bears R at a fork. The deep valley drops off sharply to the R, as easy climbing continues. At 1.0 mi, the top of a large rock outcrop provides an excellent view of Snowy Mt. to the W.

The trail soon reaches the base of a knob and circles it to the R. The summit rock outcrop is achieved at 1.2 mi. Bare rock slopes upward slightly and then sharply drops off several hundred feet to the valley floor. Be careful.

The view is outstanding. Snowy Mt. dominates to the W. Lewey and Cellar Mts. are L. The three tongues of the S end of Indian Lake are to the S. The broad bay leading to Lewey Lake is at the R. The narrow neck of Indian Lake, which receives the Jessup River, is in the middle. The beginning of John Mack Bay can be seen to the L front. An informally marked 0.5 mi trail runs E from the summit and then S to Watch Point on Indian Lake (see below).

When you return to the woods road jct. at 0.7 mi, you may wish to extend your outing by walking farther N along this grassy road. It continues as a wide lane for another 0.6 mi. The last short section swings W and descends slightly. As it begins to enter a wet area, an informal path bears L, crosses a small brook, and climbs up to the bank of NY 30 approximately 75 yd S of the S end of the Snowy Mt. parking area.

❋ Trail in winter: This is a nice little climb for snowshoers. It would be an excellent beginner's ski-shoe or snowshoe trip. It would be wise to have carefully located the trailhead in summer to be sure it can be found in winter.

🐾 Distances: To Griffin Brook, 0.1 mi; to R turnoff into woods from road, 0.7 mi; to alternate trail, 0.8 mi; to T intersection, 0.9 mi; to first lookout, 1.0 mi; to summit, 1.2 mi (1.9 km). Ascent, 357 ft (109 m). Summit elevation, 2125 ft (648 m).

Watch Hill from Indian Lake Trail (unmaintained)

Map: B2

Watch Hill has a magnificent view of Snowy Mt. and the S end of Indian Lake. The climb is short. Some care is necessary in locating the trailhead, but once found, the trail is easy to follow.

▶ Trailhead: Access to the trailhead is on the W shore of Indian Lake. The unmarked trailhead is located at the N end of a small sandy cove near Watch Point. There is a large island 0.1 mi N of Moose Island; the sandy cove, where the trailhead is located, is in a direct line with the northern third of this island and the summit of Kunjamuk Mt. Refer to your topographic map. ◀

THE TRAIL CLIMBS up a bank from the beach. There is a 10 ft high stone fireplace chimney 30 ft in the woods. It is not visible from the lake in summer. The trail heads N parallel to the shoreline, but well back in the woods. Blue blazes mark the route.

At 0.1 mi, the path crosses a rocky brook. It continues straight for 50 ft and then turns sharply L. The trail climbs very gradually. Some care is necessary in crossing rocky brook beds, but the path is generally easy to follow.

The slope becomes moderate at 0.3 mi and steep at 0.4 mi. One last steep pitch brings you to the open rock cliff summit at 0.5 mi. Snowy Mt. stands out in the W, with Lewey and Cellar Mts. to its S. The three tongues of the S end of Indian Lake are seen to the S. A trail leads N, 1.2 mi to NY 30 (trail 29).

❊ Trail in winter: The difficulty of access makes this not recommended for winter.

🐾 Distances: To brook, 0.1 mi; to steep section, 0.4 mi; to summit, 0.5 mi (0.8 km). Ascent, 475 ft (145 m). Summit elevation, 2125 ft (648 m).

(30) Snowy Mt. Trail

Map: A2–B2

Snowy Mt. is an imposing giant W of NY 30 near Indian Lake. It lacks being a 4000 ft peak by only 101 ft. The climbing ascent is 2106 ft, which is greater than that of many of the High Peaks. The summit has excellent views.

▶ Trailhead: Access to the trailhead is off the W side of NY 30, 6.9 mi S of Indian Lake village and 4.5 mi N of Lewey Lake outlet. A well-marked parking area is found on the E side of the road, opposite the trailhead. ◀

THE TRAIL IS MARKED with red DEC trail markers. It heads W up Beaver Brook Valley on a fairly level track, gaining only 267 ft in elevation before crossing Beaver Brook at 1.2 mi. A steep section, followed by a more gradual section, precedes another Beaver Brook crossing at 1.9 mi, another 180 ft higher. The trail has opened up.

The stream and several tributaries are crossed as steady climbing begins. Severe erosion is evident as the route steepens. At 3.2 mi, the trail turns R and ascends an extremely steep slope to a cliff near the summit.

The cliff offers a panoramic view of Indian Lake and beyond to the Siamese Ponds Wilderness Area. There is a spring at the edge of the woods, near where the trail continues on to the fire tower. A side trail extends 50 yd W of the spring to a lookout toward Squaw and Panther Mts. Even Mt. Morris, near Tupper Lake, can be seen beyond Panther Mt.

From the spring, the summit is 500 ft farther SW up a slight grade, at 3.9 mi. The fire tower was repaired in 2001 by members of the Student Conservation Association, part of the AmeriCorps National Service Network, and the observation cabin is open. Prominent features that can be viewed from the cabin include Indian Lake, the Siamese Ponds Wilderness, and distant mountain ranges to the E; Pillsbury Mt. to the S; Wakely Mt. to the W; Blue Mt. beyond the R shoulder of Panther Mt. to the N; and the High Peaks sweeping across the NE.

❄ Trail in winter: This is a popular snowshoe trail in winter. Its 2016 ft vertical ascent and very steep upper slopes require the same skills and equipment used for winter climbs in the High Peaks.

Distances: To first crossing of Beaver Brook, 1.2 mi; to second crossing, 1.9 mi; to R turn, 3.2 mi; to summit, 3.9 mi (6.3 km). Ascent, 2106 ft (642 m). Elevation, 3899 ft (1189 m).

(31) John Mack Pond Trail

Map: C2–C3

A boat is necessary to reach the John Mack Pond Trail, which begins at John Mack Bay on Indian Lake. From the trailhead, 175 ft of elevation will be gained and partially lost before the pond is reached.

▶ Trailhead: Access for most hikers begins at the state boat launch near Lewey Lake Public Campground and includes a paddle to the trailhead. A small island near campsite 26 on the E shore of John Mack Bay indicates you are close to the trailhead. Paddle into the small cove just beyond campsite 26 and continue to the landing at the end of the cove. A DEC signpost marks the shoreline trailhead. ◀

FROM THE TRAILHEAD (0.0 mi), the red-marked trail heads E, crosses a brook, and begins a gradual upgrade. It levels at 0.3 mi and comes along the L side of a wet zone at 0.5 mi. The trail parallels it on higher dry ground. It crosses a second brook at 0.9 mi and turns SE. Crossing two more brooks at 1.1 mi, the trail then ascends a gentle slope before the final gradual downgrade to John Mack Pond. The John Mack Pond–Long Pond Cross Trail (trail 32) jct. is reached at 1.4 mi. The Long Pond Cross Trail branches R, up a knoll to the S.

Continuing straight ahead, the trail reaches John Mack Pond at 1.6 mi. From the shore, the bulk of Kunjamuk Mt. stands out across the pond to the E. Moose Mt. is to the NW. Lily pads dot the pond and its outlet to the R. An open campsite and fire ring are found 40 ft R of the trail.

✳ Trail in winter: Due to its trailhead location, this is not a recommended trail for winter use.

🐾 Distances: To first level ground, 0.3 mi; to wet zone, 0.5 mi; to Cross Trail, 1.4 mi; to John Mack Pond, 1.6 mi (2.6 km).

(32) John Mack Pond–Long Pond Cross Trail

Map: C3

The John Mack Pond–Long Pond Cross Trail is a true wilderness trail. It is well marked with red DEC trail markers, but is more a path than a trail. It climbs through a gentle drainage area dotted with beaver dams.

▶ Trailhead: The trail begins at a jct. at the 1.4 mi point of the John Mack Pond Trail (trail 31). It climbs S over a knoll and reaches the John Mack Pond outlet at 0.1 mi. Thanks to beaver activity, the trail appears to lead right into the water (2003). However, a dry crossing is possible. Walk back on the trail 50 ft and bushwhack downstream (SW). Stay in open woods, but hug the edge of the thick spruce bordering the outlet. After a very short distance, a beaver dam can easily be crossed to the opposite shore. Walk upstream along the opposite shore until the red trail markers are again found. ◀

THE TRAIL TURNS SE and then W, as it passes over several minor grades. At 1.1 mi, the trail is high above a large beaver-affected drainage flow. At 1.2 mi, the trail descends to water level and soon approaches a large beaver house. At that point, the trail again climbs the slope and contours the valley at a higher elevation. The trail descends again when it reaches the inlet brook at the head of the beaver flow.

A gradual climb along the inlet crosses the brook three times before the trail reaches a small, unnamed, but very attractive, beaver pond at 1.8 mi. The trail again leads right into the water, but a small beaver dam across the pond outlet provides an easy way across to where trail markers can be located.

The gradual climb over Long Pond Ridge begins from this pond. The trail gradually curves to the S. As it nears the ridge line, cliffs are seen L. Height of land is reached at 2.0 mi. The trail then descends a moderate grade to the NE end of Long Pond. Here, a DEC signpost on a tree indicates the terminus of the trail at 2.2 mi. The faint Rock Pond–Long Pond Trail leads from this jct. down the W shore of Long Pond. (See trail 39, page 105.)

❄ Trail in winter: This is not recommended for winter use.

Distances: To John Mack Pond outlet, 0.1 mi; to beaver flow, 1.1 mi; to beaver pond, 1.8 mi; to height of land, 2.0 mi; to Long Pond, 2.2 mi (3.6 km). Total distance from John Mack Pond trailhead, 3.6 mi (5.8 km).

Crotched Pond Trail (unmaintained)

Map: B3

The N shore of Crotched Pond, including the peninsula, belongs to the Crotched Pond Club, and is not open to the public. To the E, a dirt road leading up a hill from Big Brook Road crosses the club's land, and should not be used to access the pond. (See trail 22, page 70.) However, the remainder of the shoreline, as well as the first 1.2 mi of the jeep road from Indian Lake, is owned by the state. With some perseverance, the state-owned shoreline can be reached via a short bushwhack from the jeep road.

▶ Trailhead: The trailhead is at the rear of campsite 14, on the E shore of Indian Lake near Crotched Pond Island. A good boat landing is found between campsites 13 and 14. A picnic site down the lake to the N, a short distance from campsite 13, makes a good place for lunch and a swim. ◀

THE UNMARKED but clear trail heads NE along the W bank of Crotched Pond Brook. It bears L and climbs up a small hill at 0.1 mi, but continues to parallel the brook. The trail drops down off the hill and meets the brook again at 0.3 mi. Both the brook and the trail then swing SE.

The valley closes in at 0.5 mi, but soon widens where a beaver dam has created a backwater. A hunter's cabin is on the L at 0.8 mi, and the trail soon begins a bend to the E, away from the brook. A beaver meadow is seen R and the trail gradually ascends.

Red paint blazes on trees on the R side of the trail at 1.2 mi mark the boundary of state lands. The remaining 0.8 mi of jeep roads leading down the peninsula to the Crotched Pond Club camp should not be traveled without permission of the owners. However, by staying on the R (W) side of the red-marked survey line, the hiker can make a 0.3 mi bushwhack on state land through the woods to the state-owned portion of shoreline. This section is not particularly good for camping, because the shoreline is lined with marsh grasses, but it does offer a nice view of Kunjamuk Mt. to the SE and of Crotched Pond Mt. to the E.

✳ Trail in winter: This trail is not recommended for winter use.

🐾 Distances: To L turn up hill, 0.1 mi; to beaver dam, 0.5 mi; to cabin, 0.8 mi; to survey blazes, 1.2 mi; to state-owned shoreline, 1.5 mi (2.4 km).

(33) Baldface Mt. Trail

Map: A3

This little mountain on the NE shore of Indian Lake provides a marvelous view of the lake. It must be approached by water. A canoe trip, mountain climb, picnic, and swim can all be part of this day trip. For those utilizing the Indian Lake Islands Public Campground, this is an excellent day activity. Vertical ascent is only 580 ft.

▶ Trailhead: The closest access is from Lakeside Cottages, on Lake Shore Drive on the W shore of Indian Lake. Lake Shore Drive is off NY 30, 4.5 mi S of the intersection of NY 30 and NY 28 in the village of Indian Lake. The other end of Lake Shore Drive is off NY 30, 1.7 mi N of the Snowy Mt. parking area. There is a large sign and marina at Lakeside Cottages. There is a small dock charge for day use of the marina. It is a paddle of approximately one mile across the lake to Normans Cove where the trailhead is located. This is 0.2 mi N of Kirpens Island, the northernmost large island in Indian Lake. ◀

THE ENTRANCE to Normans Cove is a narrow neck. A small peninsula extends from the N side of the neck. There is a public picnicking area with several tables and a fireplace.

The cove quickly widens. The trailhead is at the L rear of the cove at a large boulder and DEC sign. It is a good landing area for canoes.

The marked trail climbs a small rise through a predominantly birch forest. Red DEC trail markers guide the way. The route runs up a gradual to moderate grade in a generally SE direction. At 0.7 mi the steep wall of Baldface Mt. becomes evident. The grade becomes moderately steep as the trail begins a large horseshoe turn back to the N through red and white pines. The trail ascends steeply to open ledges on the summit at 1.1 mi.

A few blueberries can be found in season, but the panorama will keep your attention for several minutes. From R to L across the lake a sequence of mountains beckons. In the distant NW is huge, flat-topped Blue Mt. Small Porter Mt. is overshadowed by Squaw Mt. directly to your front. Panther Mt. is behind the R shoulder of Squaw, and Buell Mt. is to the rear of the L side of Squaw Mt. Farther S is the square summit of 3899 ft Snowy Mt., followed by Lewey and Cellar Mts. Finally, the Blue Ridge stretches far to the S. Floodwood Mt. is seen behind the islands and to the L of the peninsula at the W end of the lake. Below, Normans Cove sits like a jewel. A swim in the sandy-bottomed cove before the return trip is great on a hot day.

❄ Trail in winter: If the ice is thick enough, this can be a very interesting winter trip.

🐾 Distances: To trailhead via canoe, 1.0 mi; to rock wall, 0.7 mi; to summit, 1.1 mi (1.8 km). Ascent, 580 ft (177 m). Summit elevation, 2230 ft (680 m).

(34) Sprague Pond Trail

Map: Page 96

Sprague Pond is a large, attractive body of water on state land. The trail follows a firm woods road and is readily conducive to portaging a canoe.

▶ Trailhead: Access is off the N side of Cedar River Rd., 2.2 mi W of Indian Lake village. Turn off NY 28/30 and drive 4.3 mi W on Cedar River Rd. A large parking pullout is on the S side of the road and a yellow barrier gate indicates the trailhead across the road. There is no sign. If coming from Wakely Dam, the trailhead is 1.1 mi E of McCanes Resort. ◀

THE TRAIL HEADS N on a nearly level, wide woods road. At 0.4 mi, Sprague Pond can be seen through the trees. The trail curves down a gentle grade to the shore. This is an ideal picnic spot.

❄ Trail in winter: This can be an interesting little trail for an afternoon outing.

🐾 Distance: To Sprague Pond, 0.4 mi (0.6 km).

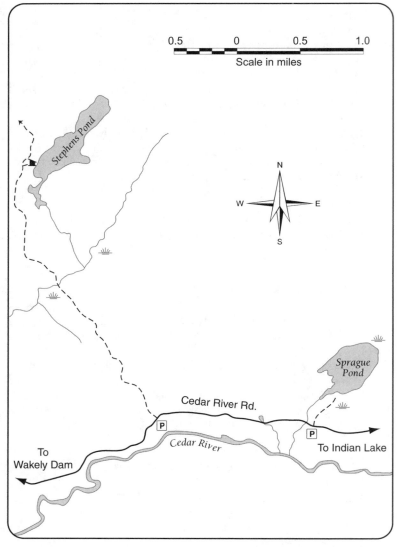

0.5   0   0.5   1.0
Scale in miles

N
W   E
S

Stephens Pond

Sprague
Pond

Cedar River Rd.

P

Cedar River

To
Wakely Dam

P

To Indian Lake

Sprague Pond and Stephens Pond from McCanes Trails
(Trails 34, 35)

(35) Stephens Pond from McCanes (N-P Trail)

Maps: Page 96 and N9, A1

The Northville-Placid (N-P) Trail currently follows the Cedar River Rd. from Wakely Dam to McCanes Resort. It then swings N to Stephens Pond.

▶ Trailhead: Trail access is off the N side of Cedar River Rd. This road is on the W side of NY 28/30, 2.2 mi W of Indian Lake village. Drive 5.4 mi on Cedar River Rd. to the trailhead at McCanes Resort. Park in the hikers' parking area provided by McCanes, on the opposite side of the road from the DEC signpost. ◀

THE TRAIL LEAVES the road at a DEC signpost (0.0 mi) in front of McCanes. It heads NW between buildings to the woods behind the woodshed. In the forest, blue DEC trail markers appear.

The trail enters state land at 0.3 mi. It gradually climbs over rolling terrain and then drops down to and crosses a vlei stream at 1.3 mi. Because the vlei is subject to flooding, it may be necessary to wade a narrow section of the brook here. An alternative is to bushwhack a short distance downstream and cross the beaver dam causing the flooding.

The route continues NW, gaining minor elevation. It crosses three more brooks and then a washout area at the end of Stephens Pond. A sign R at 2.5 mi indicates a lean-to, which sits back from the water on a rise, some 75 ft off the trail. A path leads from the lean-to to a fireplace and tent site at the shore. (For continuation of the N-P Trail to Lake Durant [trail 49] or Cascade Pond, refer to the Blue Mt. Lake section of this book and to ADK's *Adirondack Trails: Northville-Placid Trail.*)

❊Trail in winter: This is an interesting trail with opportunities for through trips in winter.

🐾 Distances: To state land, 0.3 mi; to vlei crossing, 1.3 mi; to Stephens Pond, 2.5 mi (4.1 km).

(36) Wakely Mt. Trail

Maps: Page 99 and A1

Wakely Mt. is only 256 ft short of being a 4000 ft peak. The trail ascends 1194 ft in the last 1.1 mi. The summit sports a fire tower, which is currently closed.

▶ Trailhead: Access is via Cedar River Rd. This road is off the W side of NY 28/30 on a sharp curve, 2.2 mi W of Indian Lake village. Drive along Cedar River Rd. 11.6 mi to the trailhead sign. A large parking are is on the R off the road. ◄

FROM THE TRAILHEAD (0.0 mi), walk NW along a gravel road. The red DEC trail markers are infrequent. A brief glimpse of the summit can be had at 0.3 mi. The remains of an old lumber camp are found over a bank L at 0.7 mi. The trail passes by a side road at R and then crosses a stream on a bridge at 1.1 mi. A DEC trail register is located at the crossing. The route parallels the stream for a short time before veering away.

The trail crosses two more streams before the Wakely Mt. tower sign comes into view R at 1.9 mi. The clearing visible from the jct. is the site of an old beaver pond, and is worth a brief visit. As of 1998, the dam and a large beaver lodge still were visible.

The trail turns R and climbs steeply to the summit. Yellow and red markers are intermixed on the ascent, and unmarked trails branch off the main trail at several points. A side trail to the R leads to a helipad site 240 ft from the fire tower clearing.

The summit fire tower is at 3.0 mi. Ground views are only to the SE toward Cedar River Flow.

❋ Trail in winter: Wakely Mt. is a short but rugged little climb in winter. However, from December to April, Cedar River Rd. is plowed only to a point 4.6 mi from the trailhead. Beyond, the road is a winter snowmobile trail.

❦ Distances: To first view of summit, 0.3 mi; to logging camp, 0.7 mi; to first stream crossing, 1.1 mi; to fire tower sign, 1.9 mi; to summit, 3.0 mi (4.9 km). Ascent, 1635 ft (499 m). Elevation, 3744 ft (1142 m).

Moose River Recreation Area

Map: A1

The Moose River Recreation Area is 50,000 acres of state-owned land stretching across the northern boundary of the West Canada Lakes Wilderness Area. Its eastern entrance is at Wakely Dam; its western entrance is at Limekiln Lake. While the land has been part of the Forest Preserve since 1963 (when it was purchased from the Gould Paper Co.), the 41.3 mi of roads that run throughout it are not. Through a complex conservation law, the roads were acquired as a gift for the purposes of fish and wildlife management. This has permitted development of many primitive campsites and opened them to vehicular access.

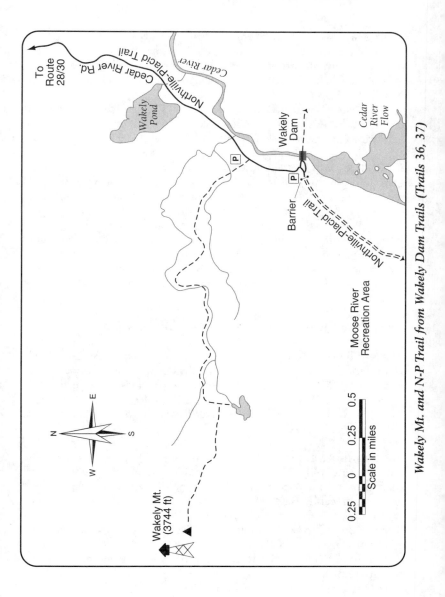

Wakely Mt. and N-P Trail from Wakely Dam Trails (Trails 36, 37)

No daily use fees have been levied in recent years, but a free permit is required if the same campsite is used for more than three continuous days. Current information can be obtained from the forest ranger at Limekiln Lake, 315-357-4403, or from the DEC regional office at Northville, 518-863-4545.

▶ Trailhead: Wakely Dam is reached via Cedar River Rd., which is off NY 28/30, 2.2 mi W of Indian Lake village. Follow Cedar River Rd. 12.0 mi to its end at Wakely Dam and Cedar River Flow. ◀

CAMPSITES AND ACCESS to Cedar River Flow are available at Wakely Dam, outside the gate to the Moose River Recreation Area. Detailed descriptions of the 27.4 mi of hiking trails in the Moose River Recreation Area are found in ADK's *Adirondack Trails: West-Central Region*. The gate at the Moose River Recreation Area normally opens for vehicular traffic on Memorial Day and closes at the end of deer season. Entry into the area on foot is permitted year round, though from December to April, the Cedar River Rd. is plowed only to a point 4.9 mi from Wakely Dam. This is a heavily used snowmobile area in winter.

(37) Northville-Placid Trail from Wakely Dam

Maps: Page 99 and A1

The N-P Trail passes through the Moose River Recreation Area at Wakely Dam. However, it is not immediately obvious how to continue S from here on the N-P Trail. This short description provides that information.

▶ Trailhead: Wakely Dam is at the outlet of Cedar River Flow, 12.0 mi along Cedar River Rd. Cedar River Rd. is 2.2 mi W of Indian Lake village on NY 28. ◀

FROM THE CARETAKER CABIN at Wakely Dam, pass through the entrance gate to the Moose River Recreation Area (see page 98). A dirt road leads 1.3 mi W to a jct., where the N-P Trail turns S. Here there is a barrier cable. Blue trail markers guide the hiker along the dirt woods road S. Vehicles can be parked in this area.

For more information about the N-P Trail, see ADK's *Adirondack Trails: Northville-Placid Trail*.

❋ Trail in winter: Refer to the Moose River Recreational Area section (page 98).

⚞ Distance: To N-P Trail barrier at jct., 1.3 mi (2.1 km).　　　　　◆

Kunjamuk Section

The Kunjamuk River enters the Sacandaga River just below Speculator. Its valley runs N to Elm Lake and on to its sources in the Siamese Ponds Wilderness Area. In the early days, the almost level "Cungemunck" valley was a principal stagecoach route to Indian Lake and was even considered for a railroad route. Its fabled cave, supposed silver mines, and logging history have all created an aura of mystique about the valley.

The S part of the valley is owned by IP. Hiking on the Speculator Tree Farm lands requires a permit. Permits can be purchased on a daily, 3 day, 7 day, 2 month, and annual basis (1997) at several places of business in Speculator or at the Speculator office of IP. Current information concerning the permit system can be obtained by calling 518-548-7931 or writing Speculator Office, International Paper Co., Box 174, Speculator, NY 12164. Camping is not permitted on IP land.

Principal access roads are East Rd., Fly Creek Rd., and Robbs Creek Rd. East Rd. is a town road; one can legally drive from Speculator to the state parking area near Cisco Creek without a permit. East Road is in good condition, and can be traveled by ordinary vehicles to within 0.3 mi of the Cisco Creek trailhead. Travel at your own risk during spring breakup, very rainy weather, or winter icy periods.

Recommended hikes in this section include the following:

SHORT HIKES:

◆ Kunjamuk Cave: 1.4 mi (2.3 km) round trip. Shrouded with mystery, this is a fascinating cave to visit.
◆ Lower Pine Lakes: 1.2 mi (1.9 km) round trip. A pleasant walk to a pair of pretty lakes.

MODERATE HIKES:

◆ Hayes Flow: 6.2 mi (10.0 km) round trip. A seldom-visited but exquisite body of water.
◆ Rock Pond and Long Pond: 5.4 mi (8.7 km) round trip. Beautiful ponds and excellent hiking once you reach the trailhead.

TRAIL DESCRIBED	TOTAL MILES (one way)	PAGE
Kunjamuk Cave	0.7 (1.1 km)	102
Lower Pine Lakes:		
North Pine Lake	0.2 (0.3 km)	103
South Pine Lake	0.4 (0.6 km)	103
Cisco Creek to the Kunjamuk River	1.2 (1.9 km)	104
Rock Pond and Long Pond	2.7 (4.4 km)	105
Hayes Flow	3.1 (5.0 km)	106

Kunjamuk Cave (unmaintained)

Map: F3

Kunjamuk Cave has been a curiosity for almost a century. The nature of its structure almost certainly indicates it was a small mine of some sort. Who made it and what, if anything, was mined there are unknown. An IP permit is required for this hike (see page 101).

At one time, it was necessary to bushwhack from an upriver bridge to reach the Kunjamuk River trailhead for the cave. In 1997, a logging bridge was built across from this trailhead. Logging operations also obliterated most of the trail from the river to the cave. The trailhead now has been moved back to Pine Lakes Rd.

▶ Trailhead: Access to the trailhead begins in Speculator, at the intersection of NY 30 and NY 8. Drive NE from the intersection on East Rd. Pavement ends at 1.5 mi, but continue on another 0.2 mi on a dirt road to a jct. Turn R onto Pine Lakes Rd. Proceed to a logging road on the R at 0.7 mi. A red pine plantation is on the R side of the Pine Lakes Rd. just beyond the logging road. Park well off the road at the intersection, being careful not to interfere with logging operations. ◀

AVOIDING A ROAD 50 yd on the L, follow the logging road 0.3 mi to the logging bridge over the Kunjamuk River at the site of the old trailhead. (If you are a paddler, it is possible to put in at Duck Bay on NY 30 and paddle via the Sacandaga River to the mouth of the Kunjamuk and then on to this point. (See ADK's *Canoe and Kayak Guide: East-Central New York State.*)

From the bridge, the road continues over a rise to a log collection yard. A logging road leaves the upper L corner of the yard, meeting the old trail on the crest of the second hill. Descending the far side of the hill, it curves R where a side trail goes L. This is 0.4 mi from the river. Take the side trail to the L and walk 100 ft to Kunjamuk Cave. The 4 ft by 4.5 ft cave entrance cuts directly into the face of Cliff Hill. A ceiling hole has been cut for sunlight. The ceiling increases from the opening to a height of 15 ft at the back of the 20 ft cave. Its walls are smooth. The many possibilities for its history are fascinating to consider.

❈ Trail in winter: While this trip is not a good one to do in winter, there are several ski trails in the Speculator Tree Farm. This is private land owned by IP. Maps can be obtained where use permits are purchased.

❦ Distances: To bridge, 0.3 mi; to Kunjamuk Cave side trail, 0.7 mi (1.1 km).

Lower Pine Lakes Trail (unmaintained)

Map: F3

The two Lower Pine Lakes are beautiful, small lakes, ringed by conifers and water plants. This trip can be combined with the Kunjamuk Cave visit to make a very nice day's outing. An IP permit is required (see page 101).

Trailhead: Trail access is identical to that for the Kunjamuk Cave (see above) up to the 0.7 mi point on Pine Lakes Rd. There, instead of taking the R fork as for Kunjamuk Cave, take the L fork. Travel 0.1 mi to the end of the red pine plantation and turn R at the road jct. The road crosses the Kunjamuk River on a wooden bridge 0.2 mi from the jct. Continue to the base of Pine Mt. where the road makes a 90° turn L (N), 1.4 mi from the jct. Park off the road at the bend. ◀

FROM THE BEND, the road continues 0.2 mi N to a camp on the R side of the road. Opposite it, a side trail L drops down to North Pine Lake. During the 150 ft walk to the lake, one's interest is aroused as the water is observed through the trees. The almost circular shoreline is edged with black spruce, tamarack, and other conifers.

At the base of a knoll opposite the bend, a washed-out road heads S into the woods. After a level stretch, a moderate upgrade begins at 0.3 mi. The road bends L and continues uphill. A bushwhack of approximately 200 yd downslope (W) from the road, after it bends L, leads to the shore of South Pine Lake at 0.4 mi. This is a pleasant place to have lunch. As in the other lake, the first signs of eutrophic decline are evident. White pond lilies float on the water.

🐾 Distances: To North Pine Lake, 0.2 mi (0.3 km); to South Pine Lake, 0.4 mi (0.6 km).

(38) Cisco Creek Trail to the Kunjamuk River

Map: D3

The Cisco Creek Trail is an excellent trail to the Kunjamuk River from the N end of the Speculator Tree Farm. The first 0.8 mi is used to reach the Rock Pond and Long Pond Trail (trail 39), and is marked with red DEC trail markers.

▶ Trailhead: The trailhead is accessed via East Rd. From the NY 30/NY 8 intersection in Speculator, drive NE on East Rd. Continue straight to a crossroads at 7.9 mi, ignoring a road that bears R at 5.1 mi. Vehicles with high road clearance can continue on to the Cisco Creek trailhead at 8.2 mi, but other vehicles should be parked well off the road at the intersection. An alternate route, Fly Creek Rd., is on IP land, and requires a fee permit to use. ◀

THERE ARE PARKING SPACES and an open campsite and fire ring at the Cisco Creek trailhead. A trail register and barrier cable are found 100 ft farther along the road.

From the trail register (0.0 mi), the trail drops down the bank, crosses Cisco Creek, and heads N. Huge white pines are seen along the trail at 0.1 mi. There is a gradual grade over a knoll and then a benchmark is embedded in a boulder R at 0.6 mi.

The Rock Pond and Long Pond Trail (trail 39) branches L at a jct. at 0.8 mi. Although USGS topographic maps may indicate a state lean-to at this jct., the lean-to no longer exists.

The trail is marked with blue DEC trail markers from this point and is easy to follow. It continues straight to the Kunjamuk River at 1.2 mi. The wide, marshy valley is very attractive. In dry seasons, the Kunjamuk is easily forded here by wading. (For the continuation of this trail, see Kunjamuk Trail, trail 22, page 70).

❄ Trail in winter: This area is frequently skied in winter. Do not expect the access road to be plowed. A day-use permit is required if one leaves the road to ski on private IP land (see page 101).

🐾 Distances: To white pines, 0.1 mi; to Rock Pond and Long Pond Trail, 0.8 mi; to Kunjamuk River, 1.2 mi (1.9 km).

(39) Rock Pond and Long Pond Trail

Map: C3–D3

Rock Pond and Long Pond are difficult places to reach from the S. Thus, they have retained a pristine quality, having suffered little abuse from humans. It is hoped that those fortunate enough to visit the ponds will do their best to preserve the natural qualities of this region. The outflows of these two ponds are source waters of the Kunjamuk River.

▶ Trailhead: Access is the same as for the Cisco Creek Trail (trail 38, above). The trailhead is at a jct. 0.8 mi along the Cisco Creek Trail. A DEC sign identifies the trail, which is marked with red DEC trail markers to the S end of Long Pond. Turn L and head N. ◀

THERE IS CORDUROY at 0.2 mi. The forest changes from mixed to open deciduous as the trail gradually gains and loses minor elevations. The trail runs along the top of a low esker-like ridge at 0.8 mi, and at 0.9 mi begins a series of undulating grade changes as it nears Rock Pond. Just after the pond comes into view ahead to the L, the trail crosses its outlet at 1.4 mi and a side trail L leads uphill along the brook to Rock Pond. The side trail ends after 100 ft at a large boulder beside the pond. A campsite is found another 100 ft N. A second side trail enters from the main trail, 250 ft beyond the outlet. This large, exquisite pond has boulders along its entire E side. Deep water is found close to shore.

A gradual uphill grade levels at 1.6 mi. After a minor depression, the route drops toward Long Pond. Rock cliffs L indicate Long Pond Ridge at 1.9 mi.

The trail arrives at the S end of Long Pond at 2.0 mi. Its S shoreline is quite rocky. The trail closely follows the W shore; several open campsites are located back from the water. The two-tiered cliffs on the opposite shore dominate the scene. Hemlock trees along the shore lend an atmosphere somewhat reminiscent of Lake George on a much smaller scale.

The trail breaks up into numerous diverging paths from the third open campsite, located at 2.3 mi, at about the midpoint of the shoreline. Take the trail closest to the water. It soon leads to a wet, brushy area.

The remaining 0.4 mi of this trail is in very poor condition. To remain dry, hikers must make a wide circle to the L, crossing a stream where it is smaller. (The careful observer may find a well-maintained spring uphill from this crossing place.) Continue to circle around to the shoreline, where a faint trail heads N. Blowdown confuses the problem, but soon the route is evident and the short distance to the N end of the pond is easily hiked. The terminus of this trail is at 2.7 mi. Here, a DEC sign on a tree indicates the John Mack Pond–Long Pond Cross Trail (trail 32).

❄ Trail in winter: This is a rugged, isolated area, seldom visited in winter. Only experienced winter campers should travel here in winter.

Distances: To corduroy, 0.2 mi; to esker-like ridge, 0.8 mi; to Rock Pond, 1.4 mi; to Long Pond, 2.0 mi; to jct. with cross trail at N end of lake, 2.7 mi (4.4 km). Total distance from Cisco Creek trailhead, 3.5 mi (5.6 km).

Hayes Flow Trail (unmaintained)

Maps: Page 107 and F3–F4

Hayes Flow is a beautiful drainage sink that collects water from a large surrounding territory. The outlet of the flow has been dammed by beavers to deepen the sink further. The result is an unusually attractive body of water, seldom visited by humans. An IP permit is required for this trail (see page 101).

▶ Trailhead: Access is on Robbs Creek Rd., off Old NY 8. The bridge at the S end of Old NY 8 is closed. To reach Old NY 8, drive 3.1 mi S from the NY 8/ NY 30 intersection in Speculator. This is 6.5 mi N from the NY 8/ NY 30 intersection N of Wells. Turn E off NY 8/ NY 30, cross the Sacandaga River bridge, and drive 1.8 mi on Old NY 8 to Robbs Creek Rd. Drive N on the hard-packed dirt Robbs Creek Rd., which crosses Robbs Creek at 1.0 mi on a heavy-duty wood bridge. The Hayes Flow trailhead is on the R, 0.1 mi past the bridge. ◀

FROM THE TRAILHEAD (0.0 mi), walk 0.1 mi E to a point where the grassy woods road veers away from Hayes Creek. Turn R onto a path that continues along the N bank of the creek. The path is the remains of an old woods road that parallels the rocky creek; it reaches Forest Preserve land at 0.4 mi.

The trail leaves the old woods road and crosses to the S side of Hayes Creek at 1.0 mi. It then continues E along the creek. An alternate route, to the R, climbs a small hill at 1.2 mi at what appears to be a dry brook bed. This route can be used in wet weather.

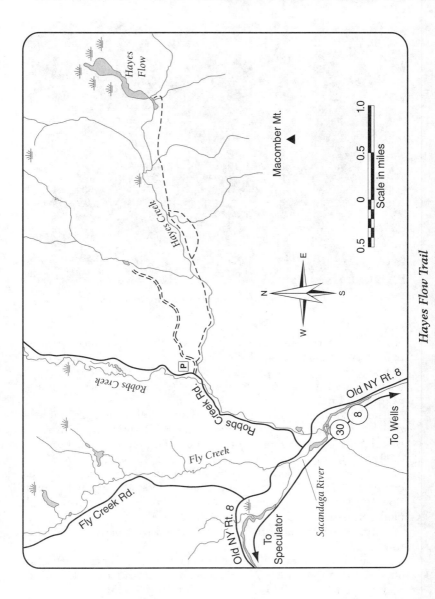

Hayes Flow Trail

Beaver activity is apparent along this trail
PHOTOGRAPH BY W. J. SCHOONMAKER

At 1.6 mi, the trail angles uphill away from the creek to avoid marshy ground farther up Hayes Creek. It crosses a small brook. Then, the faint alternate route rejoins the trail from the SW. The trail crosses another brook before passing a very large, nice, but illegal hunters' camp at 2.4 mi.

The trail heads E, soon forking R. Easy to follow until 2.7 mi, it is then much less distinct, but continues due E. The forest floor drops off sharply to the L at 2.9 mi, as the path continues to follow contours.

Hayes Flow is soon visible ahead to the L through the trees. The path drops down a slope, crosses a stream, and terminates at an open campsite near the flow at 3.1 mi. One can look NE up the beautiful flow, beyond a large beaver dam. To the NW is deep water, with a high bank across the flow.

✳ Trail in winter: This trail is difficult to follow in places. It is seldom used in winter.

🐾 Distances: To trail jct., 0.1 mi; to Hayes Creek crossing, 1.0 mi; to alternate route, 1.2 mi; to turn away from Hayes Creek, 1.6 mi; to hunters' camp, 2.4 mi; to Hayes Flow, 3.1 mi (5.0 km).   ◆

Wells to Lewey Lake Section

The first half of this section begins N of Wells, where NY 8 and NY 30 intersect. Its trails branch off NY 8/30 as it passes through the Sacandaga River valley to Speculator. This relatively narrow valley gains nearly 400 ft of elevation in about 5 mi between Auger Falls and Christine Falls. A very nice easy day's outing can be had by combining Griffin Falls (part of trail 1, page 33), Auger Falls (West), and Austin Falls. At one time Christine Falls and Whiskey Falls could have been added to the outing. However, the reopening of a hydroelectric facility at Christine Falls has closed that area to public access. The raising of the road level when NY 30 was rebuilt N of Speculator has made the stop at Whiskey Falls somewhat hazardous and probably not advisable. North of Speculator, the country is out of the confining valley and trails are more expansive. They lead through generally flat areas. There are a few small mountains. The Panther Pond Trail extends until stopped by the broad Jessup River. The Miami River Trail ends at a network of beaver dams. Other trails lead into the West Canada Lakes Wilderness Area and to the Northville-Placid Trail. In general, the hikes in this section are easy or moderate in difficulty.

Following are some recommended hikes:

Short Hikes:
◆ Auger Falls (West): 2.4 mi (3.9 km) round trip. An attractive waterfall series in a hemlock gorge awaits the hiker.
◆ Austin Falls: 0.4 mi (0.6 km) round trip. Unusual formations in the rock shoreline make this an interesting place.

Moderate Hikes:
◆ Pillsbury Mt.: 5.4 mi (8.7 km) round trip. Good views of Lake Pleasant may be had from this peak.
◆ Cedar Lakes: 8.6 mi 13.9 km) round trip. A walk into wilderness that takes you through rolling terrain and vleis.

Trail Described	Total Miles (one way)	Page
Auger Falls (West)	1.2 (1.9 km)	110
Austin Falls Walk	0.2 (0.3 km)	111
Panther Pond and Jessup River	1.7 (2.7 km)	112
Mason Lake Campsites	0.0 (0.0 km)	113
Callahan Brook	1.5 (2.4 km)	113
Pillsbury Mt.	2.7 (4.4 km)	114
Cedar Lakes	4.3 (6.9 km)	115
Pillsbury Lake	3.5 (5.6 km)	117
Pillsbury Lake To West Canada Creek	5.2 (8.4 km)	120

(40) Auger Falls Trail (West Side)

Map: Page 34

The Sacandaga River cuts sharply through the rock of a narrow gorge at Auger Falls. It is a magnificent spectacle and a place of great natural beauty. A loop trip showing the many moods of the river is possible.

▶ Trailhead: Access to the trailhead is off the E side of NY 8/30, 1.7 mi N of the NY 8 and NY 30 intersection N of Wells. Turn R into the gravel road entrance, and then immediately turn R again onto a narrow dirt road heading S. Follow this road a little over 0.1 mi to the unmarked DEC trailhead on the L, just before the road becomes a grassy lane. (The dirt road may be too rutted for a vehicle without 4WD. An alternative is to park on a widened area of the gravel road just beyond it. This adds 0.1 mi to the reported distance to the falls, but the distance for the loop as a whole remains the same.) ◀

A DEC SIGN at the trailhead states: "Warning—Hazardous Gorge Area—Sheer Cliffs—Swift Water—Slippery Footing." A trail register is located 100 ft into the woods; past it, yellow DEC trail markers become evident.

The wide, level trail swings N toward the river. At 0.3 mi, the attractive forest gives way to the river as the trail approaches the rim of the gorge. Three distinct cataracts are below, as the trail continues N through a very handsome stand of hemlocks. A large stone masonry fireplace at 0.4 mi is in view of the upper cataract. This is a good spot to have lunch.

The official trail ends here, but informal paths continue upstream, weaving around blowdown and paralleling the river as it changes to rocky rapids. At 0.9 mi, the river becomes quiet, as the trail ends at a large clearing L. (Farther upstream is a good launching site for canoeing.) The road out of the clearing leads S to the trailhead at 1.2 mi, completing the loop.

❋ Trail in winter: This could be a short snowshoe trip, but parking on NY 30 is not very safe. Visiting the falls via Auger Falls (East) Trail (trail 1, page 32) might be more advisable.

𝍩 Distances: To Auger Falls fireplace, 0.4 mi; to open clearing, 0.9 mi; to return to trailhead at end of loop, 1.2 mi (1.9 km).

Austin Falls Walk

Map: F3

In contrast to the raging torrent of Auger Falls, Austin Falls presents a small but broad waterfall. The charm of this section of river is in the potpourri of geological ocean-bottom evidence in the rock, potholes, rock channels, polished rock, and glacial striae (grooved bedrock) evident as one walks beside the fast-flowing water upstream from the falls. Both photographer and geologist will find much of interest. The falls are at roadside, so the only hiking is along the river.

▶ Trailhead: Access to Austin Falls is off Old NY 8. Turn E off NY 8/30, 6.5 mi N of the NY 8 and NY 30 intersection N of Wells. Cross the steel bridge over the Sacandaga River and drive S beside the E side of the river. Austin Falls is 2.6 mi S along this road (Old NY 8). There is a rough pullout parking space. The falls can't be seen from the road, so you must be careful to drive the exact mileage. IP has a public picnic area 0.3 mi farther along this road. ◀

THE FALLS is just a few feet off the road, but easily missed if one is not seeking it. Interesting features extend about 0.2 mi upstream from the falls.

❋ Trail in winter: This is not a good area to visit as a winter outing.

𝍩 Distance: To falls, 50 ft; upstream walk, 0.2 mi (0.3 km).

Austin Falls. RICHARD NOWICKI

Panther Pond and Jessup River Trail (unmaintained)

Map: D3

This route to the Jessup River follows an abandoned snowmobile trail on easy grades. It offers a pleasant woods walk with the added enticement of a swim in the deep river.

▶ Trailhead: Access to the trailhead is from a scenic vista parking area at Mason Lake. This is on the W side of NY 30, 7.7 mi N of Speculator. The trailhead is on the E side of NY 30, 0.1 mi S of the parking area. The trail starts at the base of a road bank and is somewhat difficult to spot. Nearby is a short wooden post which sits back 20 ft from the road. ◀

FROM THE TRAILHEAD (0.0 mi), the trail follows red tape markers SE on level terrain. Old snowmobile markers and yellow tree blazes occasionally can be spotted. The trail encounters a muddy area with deteriorated corduroy at 0.1 mi and offers a glimpse of Panther Pond N through the open woods at 0.3 mi. With some luck, red tape markers may be found leading to its shore. If not, the pond can be reached with an easy bushwhack of less than 0.1 mi on a compass heading of 30°–40°. Though an attractive pond, its marshy shoreline prevents one from getting close to its water.

Continuing on nearly level ground, the trail passes a large boulder R at 0.4 mi. At 0.6 mi the trail turns S down a gradual grade. It swings E again and climbs a short muddy section on corduroy to a height of land at 0.7 mi.

The route crosses a red-marked snowmobile trail at 0.9 mi. (To the R, the snowmobile trail leads 1.3 mi to NY 30, 0.4 mi N of the Jessup River bridge.) The trail heads SE, but soon resumes its course to the E. A short, moderate downgrade ends on the level valley floor and the trail reaches the Jessup River at 1.3 mi. The river is deep here and is approximately 100 yd wide. The mouth of Dug Mt. Brook is at a small waterfall directly across the river. A picnic area is located here.

❉ Trail in winter: With snowdrifts, it might be hard to find, and still more difficult to follow, if snowmobiles haven't recently broken trail. However, with compass, it could be a nice woods ramble.

⚞ Distances: To large boulder, 0.4 mi; to red-marked snowmobile trail, 0.9 mi; to Jessup River, 1.3 mi (2.1 km).

Mason Lake Campsites

Map: D1

Mason Lake is a small but attractive lake, visible from NY 30, 8.1 mi N of Speculator and 4.0 mi S of Lewey Lake outlet. It is on state land and has several primitive campsites on its N shore, off the road to Perkins Clearing. There is also a campsite on a small island. A pullout along NY 30 permits viewing of the lake.

Callahan Brook Trail (unmaintained)

Map: D1

At one time, this trail crossed the Miami River and climbed the shoulder of Blue Ridge along Callahan Brook. Today, Callahan Brook is a very difficult bushwhack due to beaver activity on the Miami River. At its mouth, where it enters Lewey Lake, the Miami River has always been a marsh. Over the years, the upper valley has been dammed and flooded by beavers.

▶ Trailhead: The trailhead is off the N side of the Perkins Clearing Rd. at Mason Lake. Turn W onto Perkins Clearing Rd. just N of Mason Lake, 8.1 mi N of Speculator on NY 30. Turn R into a campsite area at the top of a small hill 0.4 mi along Perkins Clearing Rd. A trail leads W from the L rear of the campsite. A red trail marker is high on an old beech tree 50 ft along the trail. Parts of the trail are marked with red tape. ◀

LONG STRETCHES of the informal path are clear; where it isn't clear, red tape markers should be kept in sight. Avoid red tape markers heading L (S) at a muddy spot at 0.1 mi. (They head back to the road.) The trail soon begins a gradual downgrade. It levels briefly at 0.4 mi before continuing to descend.

At 0.9 mi, the route turns NE. A jct., visible only because of red tape, is reached at 1.1 mi. The red tapes L head down a boggy streambed to the bank of the Miami River, where the path continues R to a beaver dam 150 yd from the jct. Beyond, beaver activity makes it very difficult to reach Callahan Brook.

The red tapes continuing straight from the jct. at 1.1 mi parallel the R bank of the Miami River N for another 0.4 mi before terminating at a bog area at 1.5 mi.

❊ Trail in winter: This is not a recommended trail for winter.

🐾 Distances: To jct. at Miami River, 1.1 mi; to terminus of trail along river, 1.5 mi (2.4 km).

(41) Pillsbury Mt.

Maps: Pages 120–121 and D1

Pillsbury Mt. is a moderately difficult climb that makes a good day trip. Its elevation is 3597 ft. There is a fire tower at the summit, but it is closed. No views can be seen from the ground.

▶ Trailhead: Access to the mountain trail is off NY 30 at Mason Lake. This is 8.1 mi N of Speculator and 4.0 mi S of the bridge over Lewey Lake outlet. Although closed from December 1 to May 1, the dirt road L (Perkins Clearing Rd.) is excellent during the remainder of the year. Follow it SW 3.3 mi to the road jct. at Perkins Clearing. The condition of the road from this point varies considerably with the season and whether lumbering operations are taking place. Be sure your vehicle is in good operating condition. The careful driver should be able to travel this route in summer without too much trouble.

Turn R from the Perkins Clearing DEC trail sign. The road passes a metal gate at 3.4 mi, and crosses a bridge over the Miami River at 4.6 mi. Sled Harbor is reached at 5.1 mi. At one time, wagons were replaced at this point and oxen were used to pull sleds up the grades ahead. Today, the area is used as a collecting point for storing logs, and considerable activity with hauling trucks periodically takes place here. The route beyond this point is still more difficult and requires good driving skills. Past Sled Harbor, one drives up a short grade and immediately reaches a road jct. Bear R and ascend a moderate grade. This short section may vary in difficulty depending on recent rainfall and maintenance. The grade and road soon improve, but are not of the quality found from Perkins Clearing. Grades steepen moderately again at 6.2 mi and the trailhead parking area and road barrier are reached at 6.3 mi. The parking area can hold 10 to 15 vehicles. ◀

THE PILLSBURY TRAILHEAD (0.0 mi) is immediately L of the trail register at the rear of the parking area.

Turning L (W), the trail immediately descends 0.1 mi to cross the Miami River, which is a small brook at this point. Once across the stream, climbing begins in earnest. The grade varies from moderate to steep for the next 1.0 mi. After passing through some minor blowdown, the trail finally levels somewhat at 1.1 mi.

At 1.3 mi, an indistinct trail jct. is found at the base of the last steep rock area before the summit. A side trail R leads 200 yd to a spring. It hasn't been used much since the fire tower ceased to be manned. Consequently, it is in poor condition. Once past the last steep section, the nearly level trail leads to the fire tower and cabin at 1.6 mi.

Views from the fire tower steps are striking. Snowy Mt. can be seen to the N, dominating Indian Lake to its E and Cedar River Flow to its W. To the W is the West Canada Lakes Wilderness Area. Pillsbury Lake and Whitney Lake are in the foreground, while Cedar Lakes can be seen in the distance beyond Pillsbury Lake. Lake Pleasant and Sacandaga Lake stand out to the S. Mountains dominate the distant horizon to the E.

✳ Trail in winter: Pillsbury Mt. is an excellent snowshoeing mountain; however, the access road is closed in the winter, and the round trip distance from Mason Lake is 15.8 mi.

🐾 Distances: To Miami River, 0.1 mi; to top of first ridge, 1.1 mi; to spring jct., 1.3 mi; to summit, 1.6 mi (2.6 km). Ascent, 1337 ft (408 m). Summit elevation, 3597 ft (1097 m).

(42) Cedar Lakes Trail

Maps: Pages 120–121 and D1

The Cedar Lakes Trail provides quick entry into the West Canada Lakes Wilderness Area. The first part of the trail is up a very pleasant woods road, which becomes a footpath for the remainder of the way to First Cedar Lake.

A small sign near the trailhead identifies this as the French Louie Trail, in honor of the colorful French Canadian trapper and guide whose main camp was at West Lake circa 1880–1915. From here to Pillsbury Lake, the French Louie Trail traces a segment of the route Louie took from West Lake to Newton Corners (now Speculator) to trade furs, stock up on supplies, and binge drink before returning to West Lake.

▶ Trailhead: For trail access, follow the same trailhead directions given for Pillsbury Mt. (trail 41, page 115). ◀

THE CEDAR LAKES TRAIL heads N up the woods road beyond the road barrier (0.0 mi) at the trail register and DEC signpost. Trailhead elevation is 2260 ft. A series of gradual grades alternating with short level sections parallels the Miami River far below to the W, between the trail and the lower slopes of Pillsbury Mt. Red trail markers are occasionally spotted. A minor dip and washed-out culvert mark a brook crossing at 0.7 mi. The way is generally easy, but a grade at 1.2 mi makes those with a heavy pack take their time. At the top of the grade, a welcome level section leads to the Pillsbury Lake jct. at 1.6 mi. Elevation is 2560 ft, 300 ft above the trailhead. (The trail L leads to Pillsbury Lake lean-to. See trail 43.)

The Cedar Lakes Trail continues straight ahead N and soon descends to Stony Brook. Here, at 1.9 mi, a skiable bridge crosses the brook and a considerable boardwalk leads to a clearing that is gradually growing in with spruce and berry bushes. The route has now become a foot-path, with little sign of the woods road width that must have existed in the past. The enjoyable route continues over almost level terrain. Grassy Brook is at 2.2 mi, where a 75 ft bridge (skiable) traverses an attractive wetland bordered by black spruces. A short, moderate upgrade at 2.4 mi crosses the end of a small ridge, before the trail grad-ually descends again to some more boardwalk. The route begins to par-allel the N side of Noisey Ridge, though the grade change is negligible.

This section is excellent in dry weather, but can become wet very quickly if it rains. The very gradual upgrade at 2.8 mi soon levels and the trail returns to lower ground. Again, a minor increase in elevation occurs at 3.0 mi and the trail then becomes almost level for a while. Minor changes in grade bring the trail to a brook crossing at 4.2 mi. There is a very brief upgrade before the concrete dam at the outlet of First Cedar Lake at 4.2 mi.

The trail formerly crossed the dam, but the crossway has washed out. The trail now turns R at the dam, drops down a slope, and crosses the Cedar River on a bridge 50 yd downstream from the dam. It then climbs up the opposite bank to the N-P Trail. A trail register is found at a jct. near the dam at 4.3 mi.

✳ Trail in winter: The winter hiker should expect to begin walking from NY 30 at Mason Lake, because the roads are not plowed unless lumbering is taking place. It is 10.6 mi from Mason Lake to First Cedar Lake. This is not a region for the inexperienced in winter. For the expe-rienced winter enthusiast, however, it provides a rugged but exciting area to explore by ski or snowshoe.

🏕 Distances: To Pillsbury Lake jct., 1.6 mi; to Stony Brook, 1.9 mi; to Grassy Brook, 2.2 mi; to Cedar Lakes dam, 4.2 mi; to N-P Trail jct., 4.3 mi (7.0 km).

(43) Pillsbury Lake Trail

Maps: Pages 120–121 and D1

Pillsbury Lake is a small, attractive lake on the first leg of a trip into the West Canada Lakes Wilderness Area. Both Whitney Lake and Sampson Lake are within day-trip range of Pillsbury Lake.

▶ Trailhead: Access is off NY 30 at Mason Lake. See Pillsbury Mt. Trail (trail 41) and Cedar Lakes Trail (trail 42) for access to the Pillsbury Lake trailhead. This trailhead is at a jct. 1.6 mi along the Cedar Lakes Trail from the parking area at the base of Pillsbury Mt. ◀

FROM THE DEC SIGNPOST at the trailhead jct. (0.0 mi), the trail follows red trail markers W down a woods road a short distance to a dip. It then climbs a long gradual grade that finally levels at 0.8 mi. The route soon gradually descends to a clearing that once had a lumber camp. There is a small informal campsite on the L at the entrance to the clearing at 0.9 mi.

The trail narrows beyond the clearing. Corduroy and boardwalks are frequent in the low, often wet area ahead. A long boardwalk crosses a wetland at 1.3 mi. After another boardwalk at 1.4 mi, what appears to be a small pond is seen through the trees to the R of the trail. It actually is the E end of Pillsbury Lake. More of the lake can be seen through the trees as the trail gradually ascends to higher ground.

Nearly level trail continues to a lean-to sign and jct. at 1.7 mi. The side trail drops a gradual 100 yd to the lean-to, which sits close to Pillsbury Lake.

❄ Trail in winter: The grades make this trail very skiable. However, the winter trailhead is generally at Mason Lake, unless late-season lumbering keeps the roads open longer than usual. Consequently, one must think in terms of a 20 mi round trip. For winter camping, this is an excellent but isolated area.

🏕 Distances: To top of first low ridge, 0.8 mi; to E end of Pillsbury Lake, 1.4 mi; to lean-to jct., 1.7 mi; to lean-to, 1.8 mi (2.9 km). From Pillsbury Mt. parking area, 3.4 mi (5.5 km).

(44) Pillsbury Lake to West Canada Creek Trail

Map: Pages120–121

This trail is a continuation of the Pillsbury Lake Trail (trail 43) into the West Canada Lakes region. Two lakes, Whitney and Sampson, can be reached from this trail, which connects into the N-P Trail. Use of this route opens up several backpacking loop routes with the N-P Trail. Though traveled relatively little until the Pillsbury Mt. parking area was opened, the trail's beauty and value are now being realized more fully by hikers.

▶ Trailhead: The trailhead is at the Pillsbury Lake lean-to jct. of the Pillsbury Lake Trail (trail 43). This is 3.3 mi from the Pillsbury Mt. parking area and 9.9 mi from NY 30 at Mason Lake. ◀

FROM THE LEAN-TO JCT. (0.0 mi), the trail continues generally W. The woods road loses elevation very slowly and the W end of Pillsbury Lake can be seen intermittently through the trees. At 0.1 mi, extensive boardwalk passes over wetland. Again, at 0.2 mi, boardwalk crosses a wetland. There is a large brook here and an abandoned beaver dam. The route passes over a small ridge and down the opposite side to a small, wet clearing on the R at 0.5 mi.

The trail continues up a rocky grade to a larger clearing on the R at 0.6 mi. This clearing is on an upslope where a building once stood. Now, various objects can be found throughout the clearing. (An informal path once led out of the upper L corner of the clearing to Whitney Lake. It no longer is traceable beyond 0.3 mi and should not be attempted.)

The woods road trail remains a gradual upgrade as it heads W. It nearly levels at 0.8 mi, reaching height of land at 0.9 mi. Then a gradual descent leads to an arrow sign at 1.0 mi, where the trail leaves the road for a short traverse through the woods to avoid a wet section. It goes over another rise at 1.2 mi.

The hiker must be careful not to miss the arrow sign at 1.5 mi on the next descent. Here, the trail turns L, off the woods road, and enters the forest. A short, moderate-to-steep downgrade ends at a brook before the trail rejoins the woods road. (At this point there is another arrow sign for hikers traveling the opposite direction.)

A very pleasant forest occupies this region. Easy rolling terrain provides enjoyable walking. Whitney Lake is seen eventually through the trees at R. (At 2.1 and 2.2 mi, informal paths once led R approximately

119

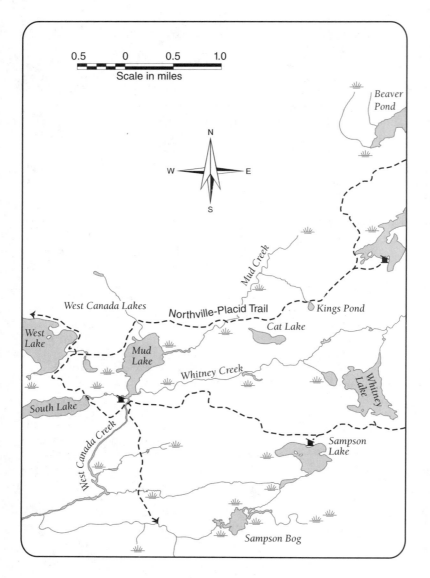

Pillsbury Mt., Cedar Lakes, Pillsbury Lake, and Pillsbury

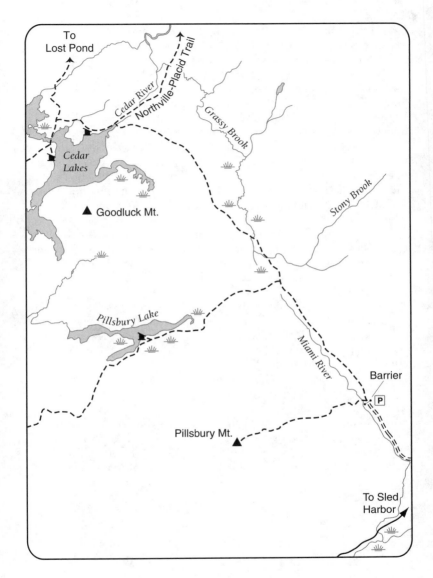

Lake to West Canada Creek Trails (Trails 41, 42, 43, 44)

0.3 mi downslope to a former camp on Whitney Lake. The paths no longer are visible, but this section of the trail parallels the lake and a bushwhack N to the lake should not be difficult.)

The descending trail soon levels, swings R, and then winds back and forth, before beginning another down grade at 2.6 mi. There is a spring on the L at 2.7 mi and soon Sampson Lake is seen through the trees. Lean-to signs on a large tree at 2.8 mi mark a jct. (This side trail leads 0.1 mi to the Sampson Lake lean-to, passing another spring on the way.)

From the lean-to jct., the trail has long gradual ups and downs before the last view of Sampson Lake at 3.1 mi. The route then levels and becomes less open. Trail signs are plentiful but brush is slowly invading the pathway. A short wet section is crossed at 3.3 mi. Soon after, the trail has a long gradual ascent up a ridge. The path then levels for a while before beginning a descent at 3.6 mi.

Crossing very gradually rolling terrain through attractive forest, the trail passes two small wet sections. The trail turns R at 4.8 mi. (There was once a cutoff trail to the N-P Trail at this point. It has not been maintained for several years and has been officially abandoned. Do not plan on using it.)

The easy rolling terrain continues to the end of Mud Lake and West Canada Creek. The trail then immediately meets the N-P Trail at a jct. at 5.2 mi. (Turning R and walking N, it is 75 ft to the bridge across West Canada Creek. The West Canada Creek lean-to is up the bank on the opposite side of the bridge.)

❄ Trail in winter: This is excellent snowshoe country and good skiing for experts. Only experienced winter campers should go into this wild area in winter.

🐾 Distances: To first arrow sign, 1.0 mi; to second arrow sign, 1.5 mi; to Sampson Lake lean-to jct., 2.8 mi; to top of ridge, 3.5 mi; to N-P Trail jct., 5.2 mi (8.4 km). This is 8.5 mi (13.7 km) from Pillsbury Mt. parking area and 14.8 mi (23.9 km) from NY 30 at Mason Lake.   ◆

Blue Mountain Lake Section

Summer campers and hikers have been coming to the Blue Mt. Lake region ever since Henry Eckford surveyed the Eckford Chain (Blue Mt. Lake, Eagle Lake, Utowana Lake) in 1811. It cost $10.00 for a stagecoach ticket from North Creek to Blue Mt. Lake in the 1870s. A traveler could reach Blue Mt. Lake from New York City in 26 hours after being conveyed by boat, train, and stagecoach. The first hotel in the world to have electric lights in every room was the Prospect House at Blue Mt. Lake. Today, the nationally recognized Adirondack Museum is found here and the village has become a center for Adirondack artists and craftspeople.

More famed for its waterways than its hiking trails, the Blue Mt. Lake region nevertheless has several fine trails. Blue Mt. and Castle Rock provide places for exquisite vistas. Many ponds offer destinations for pleasant day trips. The Northville-Placid (N-P) Trail passes E of Blue Mt. on its way to Long Lake.

Recommended hikes include the following:

SHORT HIKES:
◆ Rock Lake: 1.6 mi (2.6 km) round trip. A level walk to a pretty lake.
◆ Cascade Pond: 5.6 mi (9.0 km) round trip. An attractive combination of forest and ponds.

MODERATE HIKES:
◆ Castle Rock: 3.0 or 4.0 mi (6.5 km) round trip. Some climbing, but not too difficult. A beautiful view of Blue Mt. Lake is your reward.
◆ Tirrell Pond from Blue Mt. trailhead: 6.6 mi (10.6 km) round trip. A woods walk to a sandy beach and a very attractive pond.

HARDER HIKES:
◆ Tirrell Pond and N-P Trail: 29.6 mi (47.7 km) round trip. The N-P Trail climbs over a high ridge through wilderness country.
◆ Blue Mt.: 4.0 mi (6.5 km) round trip. A short climb with a 1550 ft ascent to the summit at 3759 ft.

Trail Described	Total Miles (one way)	Page
Sawyer Mt.	1.1 (1.8 km)	124
Rock River	3.0 (4.8 km)	125
Rock Lake	0.8 (1.3 km)	127
Tirrell Pond and N-P Trail to Long Lake	14.8 (23.9 km)	127
Stephens Pond via N-P Trail	3.3 (5.3 km)	130
Cascade Pond	2.8 (4.5 km)	131
Wilson Pond	2.9 (4.7 km)	132
Upper Sargent Pond	4.7 (7.6 km)	133
South Castle Rock (from Upper Sargent Pond Trailhead)	1.5 (2.4 km)	135
Blue Mountain Lake from South Castle Rock Trail	0.3 (0.5 km)	136
North Castle Rock (from Upper Sargent Pond Trailhead)	2.0 (3.2 km)	136
Tirrell Pond from Blue Mt. Trailhead	3.3 (5.3 km)	137
Blue Mt.	2.0 (3.2 km)	138

(45) Sawyer Mt. Trail

Map: Page 126

Sawyer Mt. is an easy climb and an excellent beginners' hike for adults or children. It has a nice view and will whet the appetite for greater challenges.

▶ Trailhead: Access is off NY 28/30 between Indian Lake and Blue Mt. Lake. A well-marked parking area is on the W side of the road 6.7 mi E of Blue Mt. Lake village. ◀

THE YELLOW-MARKED TRAIL climbs S from the parking area (0.0 mi). Rolling grades soon level off for a short time, before moderate climbing begins in a deciduous forest. After crossing an open stretch of rock, at 1.0 mi the trail turns R across sloping rock and reenters the forest. A side trail to the L, 200 ft beyond the turn, provides a lookout to the E.

The wooded summit is reached at 1.1 mi. However, the trail descends slightly to a good lookout 270 ft beyond the summit. The pond on the Wakely Lodge Golf Course is below, while Sprague Pond can be seen in the distance. Beyond (from L to R) are distant Snowy Mt., nearby Burgess Mt., Panther Mt., Wakely Mt., Metcalf Mt., rocky Sugarloaf Mt., the long Blue Ridge, and, finally, flat-topped Blue Mt. A herd path heads L (S) from the lookout toward another knob, but disappears in the woods.

❄ Trail in winter: The trail is easily reached in winter, and could be a rewarding, short snowshoe outing.

🐾 Distances: To first lookout, 1.0 mi; to summit, 1.1 mi (1.9 km). Ascent, 630 ft (192 m). Elevation, 2610 ft (796 m).

(46) Rock River Trail

Map: Page 126

The trail to Rock River was once, for the first 2.0 mi, part of the stagecoach route from North Creek to Blue Mt. Lake. Today, the route is mostly an angler's path and winter snowmobile trail. It passes through a good growth of maple and hemlock.

▶ Trailhead: Access is off NY 28/30, 6.6 mi SE of the jct. of NY 30, NY 28, and NY 28N at Blue Mt. Lake village. This is 0.1 mi W of the Sawyer Mt. trailhead. There is a well-marked parking area on the N side of the highway. ◀

FROM THE PARKING AREA (0.0 mi), the red-marked trail heads N. The trail begins a moderate descent at 0.4 mi, reaching a jct. with a red-marked snowmobile trail at the base of the slope at 0.9 mi. Crossing a small inlet of Rock Lake on a snowmobile bridge, the trail reaches a second jct. in 75 yd. It continues straight ahead and crosses a muddy stretch of lowland.

One of the bays of Rock Lake is visible through the trees L at 1.2 mi. More wetland is found at 1.4 mi. The trail climbs from the wet area and curves R at 1.5 mi.

Rock Lake can again be seen to the L at 1.6 mi. A short bushwhack will bring you to the sandy beach on its shoreline. This sandy-bottomed lake makes a fine destination if a short trip is desired. There is an excellent campsite on the N end of the lake, just E of the outlet.

The remaining distance to Rock River contours the W edge of Stark Hill on relatively level dry ground. Follow red snowmobile markers on

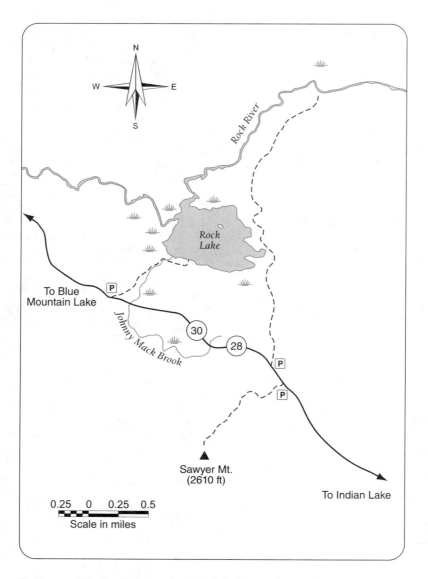

Sawyer Mt., Rock River, and Rock Lake Trails. (Trails 45, 46, 47)

this stretch of the trail. The trail descends a moderate slope at 2.9 mi and reaches the S bank of Rock River at 3.0 mi.

❄ Trail in winter: This little trail is not used much in winter but does have potential. Snowmobile trails intersect it in places.

🐾 Distances: To descent, 0.4 mi; to first view of lake, 1.2 mi; to start of bushwhack to lake, 1.6 mi; to Rock River, 3.0 mi (4.9 km).

(47) Rock Lake Trail

Map: Page 126

This is the easiest hike in the Blue Mt. region. It offers a short walk to an attractive lake, with nice mountains in the distance.

▶ Trailhead: Access is from a well-marked parking area on the N side of NY 30/28. This is 5.1 mi E from the NY 30/28/28N intersection at Blue Mt. Lake village, and 1.6 mi W of the Sawyer Mt. (trail 45, page 124) trailhead. ◀

FROM THE PARKING AREA (0.0 mi), the red-marked trail passes through a forest of red and white pines. It draws near the L bank of Johnny Mack Brook at 0.3 mi and follows it to Rock Lake. At 0.6 mi, the trail intersects a snowmobile trail with large red markers. The foot trail turns R, crossing Johnny Mack Brook on a snowmobile bridge. The foot trail bears L off the snowmobile trail at 0.7 mi, but returns to it shortly thereafter.

At 0.8 mi, the foot trail turns L, reaching a small campsite on the shore of the lake in less than 50 yd. Views of Blue Mt. (NW) and Dun Brook Mt. (N) are interesting.

❄ Trail in winter: A short trail, it provides access to Rock Lake, which could be traveled on in winter. Snowmobilers use this area.

🐾 Distances: To Johnny Mack Brook, 0.3 mi; snowmobile trail, 0.6 mi; Rock Lake, 0.8 mi (1.2 km).

(48) Tirrell Pond and N-P Trail to Long Lake

Map: M9

Tirrell Pond is a beautiful body of water with an enormous sandy beach at its NW end. There is a lean-to at each end of the pond. This waterway is somewhat overused because of its beauty and proximity to the highway. Recreationists are encouraged to carry out a little more than they carry in to help keep this area attractive. Those wishing a longer trip may continue along the N-P Trail as far as Long Lake (see ADK's *Adirondack Trails: Northville-Placid Trail*).

▶ Trailhead: The trailhead is near the Lake Durant state campground where the N-P Trail crosses NY 30/28, 2.6 mi SE of the NY 30/28/28N intersection in Blue Mt. Lake village. There is a large DEC signpost and parking area. ◀

THE TRAIL CLIMBS diagonally up the slope from the parking area (0.0 mi). It parallels the road for a short distance before turning N at 0.2 mi, following blue trail markers. Then, after a slight descent, it climbs a moderate upgrade.

At 0.6 mi, the N-P Trail veers L. (A tote road continues straight ahead on private land to O'Neil Flow.) A descent leads to two wet areas draining O'Neil Flow. The trail crosses both on good bridges and enters a Finch, Pruyn, and Co. lumbered area at 1.4 mi. An interesting rock face is seen L as the trail skirts the NW edge of O'Neil Flow.

Bearing L at a grassy area at 1.7 mi, the trail climbs away from the flow to a second grassy area and crosses a lumber road. A large brook flowing off Blue Mt. has a washed-out bridge at 1.9 mi. Just past the stream, the N-P Trail makes a sharp L and enters the woods. The trail follows the L bank and passes PBM 1883 ft at 2.1 mi. Recrossing the stream twice, the trail climbs away from the brook and crosses a lumber road at 2.5 mi.

The grade rounds off at a clearing, passes through the clearing, reenters the woods, crosses another brook, and arrives at a second clearing at 2.8 mi. The trail turns R on a good dirt road at 2.9 mi and then L onto another dirt road. It passes a slash area (2003) and reenters the woods at 3.1 mi.

State land is reached again at 3.4 mi, after another brook. Walkers Clearing is just beyond this point. O'Neil Flow lean-to is at 3.5 mi at the S end of Tirrell Pond. (Do not continue past the lean-to or across the outlet of Tirrell Pond. This leads into posted property at Wolf Pond.) The trail turns N and follows the W edge of Tirrell Pond to its NE end at 4.6 mi. Here, a beautiful crescent-shaped beach sweeps the whole end of the pond, with Tirrell Mt. on the E bank.

The trail leads a few hundred feet back from the beach to the Tirrell Pond lean-to. Many informal campsites are found at this end of the lake.

The N-P Trail turns L at the lean-to, heading W. Drinking water is found at a stream 0.2 mi W of the lean-to. The heavy use of this area by campers makes purification of the water prudent.

Beyond the stream, an unmarked trail soon leads L (it leads S and SW to lumber roads and should be avoided.) A second jct. at 4.9 mi has several DEC signs. (The yellow-marked trail L leads 3.0 mi to NY 28N, just uphill from the Adirondack Museum in Blue Mt. Lake village; see trail 54, page 137.) The N-P Trail continues straight ahead.

Beaver activity at 5.3 mi may require some wet-footed travel for a short while. The trail curves N and has a steady grade from the beaver dam. At 5.8 mi the route becomes narrower and DEC trail markers must be carefully followed. Making an abrupt L, the trail enters the woods and becomes a pleasant footpath. It levels off and crosses a tote road at 6.1 mi. After a slight descent, it crosses a swampy area at 6.5 mi. Continuing N, the old tote road crosses a lumbered area that is quite barren and arrives at a jct. with the Salmon Pond gravel road at 7.0 mi.

Turn R (E) and follow this road. It crosses the Salmon River bridge at 7.2 mi; several informal campsites are located here. From there, it climbs a grade to another road jct. at 7.4 mi.

The trail turns L at the jct., heading NW. This section of the trail becomes progressively more comfortable and is soon very enjoyable. It gradually but steadily ascends the ridge. An interesting ravine is seen to the L at 8.5 mi. Then, at 8.6 mi, the trail crosses a brook; considerable flooding due to beaver activity may be encountered at a large clearing.

Another small clearing is found at 8.9 mi and the trail turns sharply L, continuing to climb. It swings N just before passing a third clearing. The route bears L at 9.3 mi and climbs upward. A good cold spring is on the L at 9.7 mi; soon after, the trail crosses a brook at 9.8 mi. The trail turns E and climbs a steep pitch at 10.1 mi. The ridgeline is achieved at 10.2 mi; the elevation is 2980 ft. This seldom-traveled section of trail is fern-covered and most rewarding. The trail now swings E and climbs to a little over 3000 ft in elevation as it crosses over the height of land.

Turning NE, the trail begins a rapid descent at 10.6 mi. The grade moderates at 11.0 mi, but continues to descend at a lesser rate to a lumber clearing at 11.4 mi. Still descending, it crosses Sandy Creek on a bridge at 12.3 mi and begins to level out. It joins the dirt Long Lake Reservoir Rd. at 13.2 mi. There is a cable barrier at this jct.

The route again swings N at 13.7 mi and recrosses Sandy Creek on a bridge at 14.0 mi. The next half mile crosses a swampy section, but one of the most extensive log bridging projects in the Adirondacks keeps you dry. This section is very well maintained.

The route climbs up a small grade to a parking area and NY 28N at 14.8 mi. This point is 1.5 mi E of Long Lake village. (A more detailed description of this route is available in ADK's *Adirondack Trails: Northville-Placid Trail*.)

❆ Trail in winter: This can be an excellent ski trip to Tirrell Pond, perhaps as part of a trip through to NY 30 near the Adirondack Museum via the Tirrell Pond and N-P Trail from Blue Mt. Trail (trail 55, page 138).

⚸ Distances: To O'Neil Flow lean-to, 3.5 mi; to Tirrell Pond lean-to, 4.6 mi; to jct. at beginning of Blue Ridge climb, 7.4 mi; to height of land on ridge, 10.2 mi; to NY 28N, 14.8 mi (24 km).

(49) Stephens Pond via N-P Trail

Map: N9

Stephens Pond is a pretty little pond with a lean-to. It is visited principally by backpackers on the N-P Trail, but also makes a nice day trip.

▶ Trailhead: Access is from NY 28/30 at Lake Durant state campsite, 2.6 mi SE of the NY 30/28/28N intersection in Blue Mt. Lake village. A large DEC sign marks the point where the N-P Trail crosses the highway; ample parking space is provided on each side of the road. By parking here, rather than driving into the campsite, one is not required to pay a day-use fee. ◀

LEAVING THE HIGHWAY (0.0 mi), the route climbs the bank from the parking zone on the S side of NY 28/30, following blue trail markers. It crosses Rock River on a bridge, then turns R and crosses the parking area near the bathing area.

Follow the paved road S from the parking area. Passing over the Stephens Pond outlet bridge, the route turns L at 0.4 mi onto the campground truck road at campsite number 3. A gradual upgrade leads to a jct. at 0.8 mi. The road turns L up a hill. Continue straight ahead. Another jct. with a DEC trail register is reached at 0.9 mi. The unmarked trail R heads back to the campground road. The route passes through an open grassy area at 1.0 mi.

The trail continues SW at a gradual incline to a jct. at 2.7 mi. (The red-marked trail R leads 0.9 mi to Cascade Pond [trail 50]). The N-P

Trail goes down an incline to the L, descending 150 ft before reaching Stephens Pond. A side trail L at 3.3 mi leads 85 ft to the Stephens Pond lean-to. (The N-P Trail continues S, 2.5 mi to McCanes Resort on Cedar River Rd. and 9.1 mi to Wakely Dam; see Indian Lake Section, page 95.)

The pond has a variety of birds and water life. Beavers have dammed up its S end and have a large house along the shore. To the N, a 3000 ft ridge is prominent.

❊ Trail in winter: This is an excellent ski route, which can be combined with the Cascade Pond Trail (trail 51, page 132) and then a ski down Lake Durant to complete a loop.

⚑ Distances: To campground truck road, 0.4 mi; to first jct., 0.8 mi; to DEC register, 2.7 mi; to Stephens Pond lean-to, 3.3 mi (5.3 km).

(50) Cascade Pond Trail

Map: N8–N9

The Cascade Pond Trail has an unusual variety of water and forest settings of great beauty. It can be combined with the Stephens Pond Trail (trail 49) to make a loop trip, but this requires a car at each trailhead.

▶ Trailhead: The trailhead is reached by driving E on NY 28/30 from the NY 30/28/28N intersection in Blue Mt. Lake village. Turn R onto Durant Rd., 0.9 mi from the intersection, then travel 0.2 mi to the small trailhead sign on the L at a narrow dirt road. This is just before a cemetery. Parking is at the edge of the road. ◀

FROM THE TRAILHEAD (0.0 mi), red DEC trail markers lead to a DEC sign at 0.1 mi identifying a R turn. A small brook is crossed as the path heads W.

At 0.6 mi, a small decline leads to a 200 ft bridge across Rock Pond. This is a very attractive body of water. Across the bridge, a short, steep section heads S to the top of a minor ridge. The trail then descends steeply to a valley floor, crossing a stream at 1.1 mi.

Traveling W again, the route wends its way up a beautiful wooded valley. There is a brief incline at 1.8 mi as the trail climbs up to level ground. At 2.3 mi, the trail turns L at a DEC sign and heads E. The tree type is now mostly spruce. The trail narrows as it approaches Cascade Pond. The Cascade Pond lean-to is at 2.8 mi, next to the pond's outlet. It has a commanding view of the pond. (The trail crosses the outlet and continues around the E side of the lake another 0.9 mi to the jct. with the N-P Trail, 0.6 mi N of Stephens Pond.)

✳ Trail in winter: Refer to Stephens Pond from Lake Durant campsite (trail 49, page 130).

𝍂 Distances: To Rock Pond, 0.6 mi; to stream crossing, 1.1 mi; to end of valley, 1.8 mi; to jct., 2.3 mi; to Cascade Pond, 2.8 mi (4.5 km).

(51) Wilson Pond Trail

Map: N8

Wilson Pond is an attractive body of water in the Blue Ridge Wilderness Area. The trail exhibits considerable variety in both conditions and flora. There is a lean-to at the pond.

▶ Trailhead: The trailhead is off the SE side of NY 28, opposite Eagle Lake. At a point 2.8 mi W of the jct. of NY 28, NY 28N, and NY 30 in Blue Mt. Lake village, there is a small parking area. The trailhead sign (0.0 mi) is located a few feet into the trees. ◀

RED DEC TRAIL MARKERS indicate the route SE through balsam fir and other conifers. The way is muddy in spots. A path cuts across the trail at 0.3 mi. The trail crosses Grass Pond outlet at 0.5 mi. The small pond, on the L, has many tamaracks around its shore.

At 0.7 mi, the route crosses the outlet stream of Long Pond, which flows through a wetland with open water lying to the R. After passing through a field of ferns, the trail then crosses another wetland zone as it negotiates the Slim Pond outlet. Corduroy and a bridge ease the difficulty of travel. At the far end of the wet area a side trail to the L leads to a spring. In times of heavy rain, this area may flood, making passage impossible.

The trail gains elevation to drier ground gradually over the next 0.4 mi, and enters an open hardwood forest. It crosses Wilson Pond outlet at 1.8 mi. The pond is to the L past a marshy area, but the trail circles around it on higher dry ground. Vegetation is again coniferous.

The route turns L at 2.5 mi, heading NE. It again crosses Wilson Pond outlet at 2.7 mi. The trail then enters a stand of spruce trees and comes to Wilson Pond lean-to at 2.9 mi.

The pond has boggy growth and is surrounded by conifers. An island is not far from the lean-to. There is a rocky ledge at the water's edge, and Blue Ridge is across the water to the S.

❅ Trail in winter: This trail is little used in winter but can be excellent if conditions are good.

🐾 Distances: To Grass Pond, 0.5 mi; to Long Pond, 0.7 mi; to first crossing of Wilson Pond outlet, 1.8 mi; to second crossing of Wilson Pond outlet, 2.7 mi; to Wilson Pond lean-to, 2.9 mi (4.7 km).

(52) Upper Sargent Pond Trail

Maps: Page 134 and M8

Upper Sargent Pond has long been used for fishing. Guides had fishing camps there in the heyday of the Adirondack hotels in the 1800s. The trail to Upper Sargent Pond is relatively level past the initial upgrades, and passes through deciduous forest.

▶ Trailhead: Access is off NY 30/28N. Turn L onto Maple Lodge Rd., 0.6 mi N of the NY 30/28/28N intersection in Blue Mt. Lake village. Drive 1.3 mi along a paved and then gravel road to the DEC trailhead sign beside the Minnowbrook Conference Center control station. Minnowbrook has provided a long pullout for trailhead parking on the L just before the control station. If this is full, the closest parking is 1.3 mi back on NY 30/28N. ◀

FROM THE TRAILHEAD (0.0 mi), head W on a private road. Bear R uphill at a fork at 0.2 mi. There is another DEC trail sign on the R side of the road at 0.3 mi. Here, the trail leaves the road and enters the woods, following red DEC trail markers. The road straight ahead enters private land and should be avoided.

The trail reaches a jct. at 0.4 mi. L is the South Castle Rock Trail (trail 53), the first of two trails to Castle Rock. Continue straight.

The trail passes E of Chub Pond at 0.7 mi and then generally swings W. At a jct. at 1.5 mi, the trail L is the North Castle Rock Trail (trail 53B). It follows yellow markers 0.5 mi to the summit of Castle Rock.

The trail now parallels the N edge of a wetland on dry ground for nearly a mile. Helms Pond is to the N, but is not visible. At 3.1 mi, the trail descends to the level of another wetland, where it meets the outlet of Helms Pond. The trail hugs the S side of the outlet all the way to Upper Sargent Pond, passing through large stands of yellow birch and sugar maple.

The pond is reached at 4.7 mi. The informal campsite at the trail terminus is surrounded by large conifers.

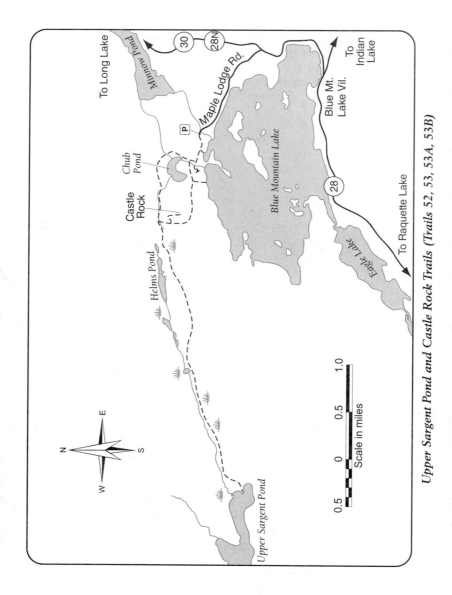

Upper Sargent Pond and Castle Rock Trails (Trails 52, 53, 53A, 53B)

For other access to Upper Sargent Pond, see ADK's *Adirondack Trails: Northern Region.*

❄ Trail in winter: Limited parking at the trailhead in winter makes use of the trail difficult, but the trail itself is excellent.

🐾 Distances: To turn off road, 0.3 mi; to South Castle Rock Trail, 0.4 mi; to Chub Pond, 0.7 mi; to North Castle Rock Trail, 1.5 mi; to outlet of Helms Pond, 3.1 mi; to Upper Sargent Pond, 4.7 mi (7.6 km).

(53) South Castle Rock Trail

Maps: Page 134 and M8

Castle Rock juts 200 ft above the surrounding forest trees like a medieval castle. It offers a magnificent view of both Blue Mt. and Blue Mt. Lake. There are two trails to its summit, one approaching from the S (trail 53) and the other from the N (trail 53B). Both branch off the Upper Sargent Pond Trail (trail 52), making round trips of 3.0, 3.5, or 4.0 mi possible.

▶ Trailhead: Access is the same as that for Upper Sargent Pond (trail 52). Follow the Upper Sargent Pond route from its trailhead for 0.4 mi to the jct. mentioned in the Upper Sargent Pond trail description. ◀

THE YELLOW-MARKED TRAIL heads W across a bridge (0.0 mi). It bears R off the woods road at 0.1 mi, continuing on easy grades. Chub Pond can be seen R at 0.3 mi. Shortly thereafter, the trail turns SW, following a stream down a gradual grade to a jct. at 0.4 mi. The blue-marked trail L heads down to Blue Mt. Lake (trail 53A).

The trail continues W from the jct. on the level, but the grade soon increases to moderate and then steep. At 0.6 mi, the trail turns NW on easy to moderate grades. It drops down into a hollow at 0.8 mi, then ascends a short, steep pitch along the S face of Castle Rock to an overhang R at 0.9 mi. (A herd path heads R at the overhang, meeting up with the yellow-marked trail again part way up the W face.)

From the overhang, the trail heads NW on easy to moderate grades to a jct. at 1.0 mi. The yellow-marked trail L is the North Castle Rock Trail (trail 53B). Turning R, the trail heads steeply up the W face of Castle Rock, and reaches the top at 1.1 mi. See the North Castle Rock Trail (53B) for a description of the view.

❄ Trail in winter: **Caution: Extreme care is urged. The upper part and lookout ledge are quite dangerous in winter.**

꛳ Distances: To Blue Mt. Lake Trail jct., 0.4 mi; to overhang, 0.9 mi; to jct. with North Castle Rock Trail, 1.0 mi; to summit, 1.1 mi (1.8 km). Total distance from Upper Sargent Pond trailhead, 1.5 mi (2.4 km). Ascent from Upper Sargent Pond Trail, 580 ft (177 m). Summit elevation, 2480 ft (756 m).

(53A) **Blue Mountain Lake from South Castle Rock Trail**
Maps: Page 134 and M8

This short trail can be used as a pleasant side trip on the way to or from Castle Rock, or to climb Castle Rock from the lake.

▶ Trailhead: Access is the same as for the South Castle Rock Trail (trail 53). The trailhead is at a jct. 0.4 mi along the South Castle Rock Trail. If approached from the lake, the trail can be accessed by circling around the W side of Bluff Point. The W tip of Long Island is directly S of the landing. A DEC trail sign is posted on a tree at the shore. ◀

THE BLUE-MARKED TRAIL heads S down a gradual grade beside a stream, passing by the ruins of a stone structure in the middle of the stream before reaching Blue Mt. Lake at 0.3 mi. A small clearing and sandy beach mark the terminus. Long Island and other small islands are straight ahead.

✳ Trail in winter: Unlikely to be a destination in and of itself in the winter, the trail could be used as part of a ski trip across the lake and snowshoe climb of Castle Rock. **Caution: As noted elsewhere, extreme care is advised at the top of Castle Rock**.

꛳ Distances: To Blue Mt. Lake, 0.3 mi (0.5 km). Total distance from Upper Sargent Pond trailhead, 1.1 mi (1.8 km).

(53B) **North Castle Rock Trail**
Maps: Page 134 and M8

This route to Castle Rock from the Upper Sargent Pond trailhead is longer than the route from the S (trail 53). However, combining the trails in a loop adds variety to the round trip and only 0.5 mi to the total distance.

▶ Trailhead: Access is the same as that for Upper Sargent Pond (trail 52). Follow the Upper Sargent Pond route from its trailhead for 1.5 mi to the jct. mentioned in the Upper Sargent Pond trail description. ◀

FROM THE JCT. (0.0 mi), the yellow-marked trail climbs S and E to a jct. at 0.4 mi. The South Castle Rock Trail (53) enters R. Turning L, the trail to the summit climbs steeply up the W face of Castle Rock.

Passing through a corridor with a high rock wall, the trail reaches the summit at 0.5 mi. Here, it breaks out onto a large, flat, open rock platform overlooking Blue Mt. Lake. The summit is 700 ft above the water level. Green islands stand out of the blue water below like emeralds in ice. To the E, Blue Mt. dominates. Far on the horizon to the SW is Snowy Mt. near Indian Lake. Lake Durant (SE) and Eagle Lake (SSW) are visible. Helms Pond is to your right rear (WNW).

❄ Trail in winter: **Caution: Extreme care is urged. The upper part and lookout ledge are quite dangerous in winter.**

🐾 Distances: Trailhead to jct. with South Castle Rock Trail, 0.4 mi; to summit, 0.5 mi (0.8 km). Total distance from Upper Sargent Pond trailhead, 2.0 mi (3.2 km). Ascent from Upper Sargent Pond Trail, 380 ft (116 m). Summit elevation, 2480 ft (756 m).

(54) Tirrell Pond from Blue Mt. Trailhead

Map: M9

The trail to Tirrell Pond from the Blue Mt. trailhead passes through private woods and circles the base of Blue Mt. from the N. The forest was lumbered a few years ago, but is recovering. Young growth sometimes closes in on the trail, but generally the way is open and quite pleasant.

▶ Trailhead: Access is off the E side of NY 30/28N, 1.4 mi N of the NY 30/28/28N intersection in Blue Mt. Lake Village. This trailhead is at the top of the hill, 0.1 mi N of the Adirondack Museum. There is ample parking available at this dual trailhead. ◀

THE YELLOW-MARKED TRAIL leaves the highway (0.0 mi) and heads N. The route is almost level as it gradually swings to the E. A break in the deciduous growth occurs at 0.5 mi, when the trail passes through a power line right-of-way. NY 30/28N can be seen far downhill to the L. Half grown-in old lumber roads frequently cross the trail, but offer no confusion. A large flat boulder sits on the L at 1.2 mi. A well-maintained dirt road crosses the trail at 1.6 mi.

At the low col between Blue Mt. and Buck Mt., it is possible to glimpse each peak occasionally. The 470 ft vertical descent to Tirrell Pond begins at 2.1 mi. The trail crosses two sets of grassy logging roads at 2.4 mi. The descent steepens somewhat, and the eroded path has many loose cobblestones at 3.1 mi. Then, the route levels before coming along the L bank of a brook.

The trail crosses a branch of the brook 60 yd before reaching the jct. of the N-P Trail at 3.0 mi. Several DEC signs are found on trees. Turn R for Tirrell Pond. (The N-P Trail L goes N 9.9 mi to Long Lake.) Avoid an unmarked side trail to the R a short distance farther along the trail.

The trail crosses a large brook at 3.1 mi and reaches Tirrell Pond lean-to at 3.3 mi. The N end of the pond is several hundred feet in front of the lean-to. Its crescent beach and attractive Tirrell Mt. to the E make the pond an oft-visited area. Please be careful to carry out everything you carried in to this beach, so future hikers will be able to enjoy its environment.

❋ Trail in winter: This trail is best skied heading E. It is often combined with the N-P Trail out to Lake Durant (trail 48).

𐄷 Distances: To power line right-of-way, 0.5 mi; to dirt road, 1.4 mi; to downgrade, 2.1 mi; to N-P Trail jct., 3.0 mi; to Tirrell Pond lean-to, 3.3 mi (5.3 km).

(55) Blue Mt. Trail

Map: M9

First named To-war-loon-da, the Hill of Storms, by the Iroquois, this mountain was then named Mt. Clinch, after a state assemblyman who supported the Eckford survey of 1811. (The lake was named Lake Janet, after Eckford's daughter.) Fortunately, the many thousands of annual visitors to this area don't have to climb Mt. Clinch from Lake Janet. Instead, beautiful Blue Mt. is the name of the summit from which Verplanck Colvin's men set off their bright explosions at night to permit Adirondack Survey crews to zero in their triangulation points. Perhaps because it is so accessible from a major highway, and earlier was near a hub of hotels, Blue Mt. has been one of the most frequently climbed Adirondack peaks for over a century.

▶ Trailhead: Access coexists with the Tirrell Pond trailhead on NY 30/28N, 1.4 mi N of the NY 30/28/28N intersection in Blue Mt. Lake village. This is 0.1 mi up the hill past the Adirondack Museum on the E side of the road. There is ample parking at the trailhead on private property. ◀

THE TRAIL HEADS E from the parking area following red trail markers. (Avoid the yellow-marked DEC trail heading N to Tirrell Pond; see trail 54.) A barrier cable blocks vehicular use. The flat logging road swings SE and then gradually gains elevation. At 0.2 mi,

Blue Mountain. PHOTOGRAPH BY VINCENT P. LONG

the trail enters woods, soon crossing a creek. Elevation continues to be gained at a comfortable rate.

At 0.9 mi, a moderate grade soon eases. Then, the route steepens until it climbs over bare rock sheets. The grade finally levels at 1.5 mi and heads NE through attractive spruce.

The last half-mile is very enjoyable and ends at the summit at 2.0 mi. Good views are to be had from the flat-topped summit at ground level, but excellent views are the reward for climbing the fire observer's tower. To the W is Blue Mt. Lake. To its L are Eagle Lake and beyond it Utowana Lake. Beyond the ridges, Raquette Lake is visible. To the N are Minnow Pond, Mud Pond, South Pond, and finally part of Long Lake. In the NE, Tirrell Mt. with beautiful Tirrell Pond is below. Just to the L is Tongue Mt. Algonquin Mt. (second highest in the Adirondacks), 25 mi to the NE in the High Peaks, is in line with Tongue Mt.. To the R of the gap by Algonquin are Avalanche Pass and then Mt. Colden. Somewhat farther L of Algonquin are Ampersand Mt. and the Seward Range. Much closer is Kempshall Mt. on the E shore of Long Lake.

❄ Trail in winter: Blue Mt. is an excellent winter climb. Instep or full crampons are recommended for this trip.

🐾 Distances: To beginning of steeper grades, 0.9 mi; to level area, 1.5 mi; to summit, 2.0 mi (3.2 km). Ascent, 1550 ft (473 m). Summit elevation, 3759 ft (1146 m). ◆

Stony Pond Lean-to.
PHOTOGRAPH BY BRUCE C. WADSWORTH

Olmstedville-Newcomb Section

The Olmstedville-Newcomb section is one of those seldom-traveled parts of the Adirondack Park, seemingly unknown to the general hiking public. Hikers bypass it on the E as they head up the Adirondack Northway (I-87) to the High Peaks. Campers miss it on the W as they travel up NY 30 through the lake county. All of this has resulted in an island of noncommercial Adirondack country treasured by those who know it for its beauty, solitude, and true Adirondack atmosphere.

This has always been timber country. It was state Assemblyman Wesley Barnes of Olmstedville who championed the legislative bill that created the Forest Commission in 1885. The Forest Commission became the Conservation Department, which in turn became today's Department of Environmental Conservation.

The destinations in this section range from the Blue Ledges on the Hudson River, to the waters of Stony Pond country, to the vistas of the High Peaks from Goodnow and Vanderwhacker Mts. There are many private clubs in this section. Their private trails appear on topographic maps. The hiker is cautioned to obtain permission before walking private trails that are not described in this guide.

Recommended hikes in this section include:

SHORT HIKES:
◆ Boreas River: 2.4 mi (3.9 km) round trip. A charming walk along the Boreas River.
◆ Newcomb Visitor Interpretive Center: Three trails offer very interesting recreational and educational opportunities.

MODERATE HIKES:
◆ Goodnow Mt.: 3.8 mi (6.1 km) round trip. A superior view for very little effort.
◆ Blue Ledges: 5.0 mi (8.1.0 km) round trip. A woods walk to one of the most beautiful parts of the Hudson River.

HARDER HIKES:

- Hewitt Pond to Irishtown: 15.8 mi (25.5 km) round trip. Travel from pond to pond through magnificent forest, on the Stony Pond from Hewitt Pond and Stony Pond from Irishtown trails.
- Vanderwhacker Mt.: 5.4 mi (8.7 km) round trip. Climb a mountain for a panoramic view of the High Peaks.

TRAIL DESCRIBED	TOTAL MILES (one way)	PAGE
Stony Pond Country		
Stony Pond from Hewitt Pond	4.0 (6.5 km)	143
Center Pond	0.2 (0.3 km)	144
Stony Pond from NY 28N	2.1 (3.4 km)	145
Stony Pond from Irishtown	3.9 (6.3 km)	145
Blue Ledges	2.5 (4.0 km)	147
Rankin Pond	0.4 (0.6 km)	149
Linsey Marsh	2.0 (3.2 km)	149
Boreas River	1.2 (1.9 km)	150
Hewitt Eddy	0.8 (1.3 km)	151
Vanderwhacker Mt.	2.7 (4.4 km)	151
Santanoni Preserve		154
Newcomb Visitor Interpretive Center		156
Goodnow Mt.	1.9 (3.1 km)	157

Stony Pond Country

Stony Pond is actually a lake. It has an irregular shoreline of immense length. Green Mt., to the E, is a good bushwhack trip and an even better snowshoe destination in winter.

The collection of small ponds and lakes north of Irishtown offers a great variety of opportunities to the hiker. A day trip to Stony Pond can begin at any of three trailheads: Irishtown, NY 28N or Hewitt Pond. A through trip from Hewitt Pond S to Irishtown can be a long day hike or a more leisurely backpack or fishing trip. The trail to Stony Pond from NY 28N makes a pleasant afternoon outing or can be the beginning of an interesting day hike to Irishtown.

(56) Stony Pond from Hewitt Pond Trail

Map: 17

The trail from Hewitt Pond to Stony Pond is lightly used and over-grown in places. Be sure to keep track of the last trail marker while searching for the next one. However, persistence is amply repaid by the nice combination of ponds, a bog, and open woods along the route.

▶ Trailhead: The Hewitt Lake Club Rd. to the trailhead turns E off NY 28N at Aiden Lair. (While the club refers to itself as the Hewitt Lake Club, the USGS map refers to the body of water as Hewitt Pond and its neighboring mountain as Hewitt Pond Mt.) This is 6.6 mi N of the NY 28N/Olmstedville Rd. intersection in Minerva and 1.9 mi S of the Boreas River bridge. The level dirt road leads 0.5 mi to a large parking area on the S side of the road, just before the gateway to the Hewitt Lake Club. ◀

THE TRAIL LEAVES the corner of the parking area, following red DEC trail markers. A gentle downslope leads 100 ft to a 400 ft boardwalk over a wet area. The Hewitt Lake Club property line appears on the L at 0.2 mi. The posted shoreline of Hewitt Pond is visible through the trees.

At 0.3 mi, the trail climbs a small grade to a height of land. Dropping down more steeply, it reaches the shoreline of Hewitt Pond again at 0.6 mi. The trail follows the shoreline, which at this point is part of the state-owned Forest Preserve. Hewitt Pond Mt. can be seen N across the pond.

Gradually pulling away from the pond, at 0.8 mi the trail turns R at a large downed tree (1999). (The tree covers a jct., the L fork of which continues beyond the blowdown.) The trail crosses a brook at the remains of a small bridge at 1.0 mi. The route follows the brook for a short distance, and then turns from S to SE as it leaves the brook and ascends a gradual grade.

The trail reaches the thickly tree-lined E shore of Barnes Pond at 1.7 mi. A fast-moving inlet stream is crossed and soon the trail leaves the pond to begin the long upgrade that terminates at the beginning of the Stony Pond watershed. Height of land is at 2.3 mi, after an ascent of 370 ft.

The descent is less steep than was the climb. At 2.7 mi a bog meadow with a small pond at its far end comes into view. The trail follows its E border to a jct. at 3.1 mi. Here, a DEC trail with yellow markers goes L and cuts 0.2 mi E over a low ridge, dropping down to Center Pond (see trail 57).

The trail follows the outlet of the pond to the NE corner of Stony Pond at 3.3 mi. Crossing the brook, the trail heads back upstream 40 yd before turning sharply N and climbing a ridgeline. From the height of land the trail descends SW and crosses a brook at 3.6 mi. The route follows an open woods road from this point and pulls away from Stony Pond to bypass a peninsula.

Stony Pond Brook, the outlet of Stony Pond, is reached at 4.0 mi, where it cuts through a rock zone. The Stony Pond lean-to is just out of sight on the opposite bank.

Beavers may have added to the natural dam at the outlet, making its crossing somewhat difficult. If so, a drier crossing may be found over one of the smaller beaver dams downstream. After crossing, find a woods road from NY 28N and follow it uphill to the lean-to, which occupies a very picturesque setting.

✤ Trail in winter: This is a very difficult trail for skiers.

🐾 Distances: To Hewitt Pond, 0.2 mi; to Barnes Pond, 1.7 mi; to top of ridge, 2.3 mi; to Center Pond Trail jct., 3.1 mi; to NE end of Stony Pond, 3.3 mi; to Stony Pond lean-to, 4.0 mi (6.5 km).

(57) Center Pond Trail

Map: 17

Center Pond is an attractive body of water surrounded by a fairly open forest and shoreline. A trail from Little Sherman Pond was apparently abandoned when the trail to Stony Pond from Hewitt Pond was developed.

▶ Trailhead: Follow the directions for the Stony Pond from Hewitt Pond Trail (trail 56) to a trail jct. at the 3.1 mi point. ◀

THE TRAIL IS NOT IDENTIFIED by a sign and is overgrown in places. However, yellow DEC trail markers are plainly visible at the jct. and can be easily followed to the pond. They lead L (E) up a moderately steep ridge. The grade soon levels. A few minutes' walk brings you to a steep downgrade and the shore of Center Pond at 0.2 mi.

✤ Trail in winter: This is very difficult to ski, but might be a short snowshoe trip for campers at the Stony Pond lean-to.

🐾 Distances: To Center Pond, 0.2 mi (0.3 km). Total distance from trailhead, 3.3 mi (5.3 km).

(58) Stony Pond from NY 28N

Map: 17

This is the shortest route to Stony Pond. The trail follows an old woods road over easy up-and-down grades. Its course is part of a snowmobile trail to Irishtown. In summer, it makes a delightful afternoon hike.

▶ Trailhead: Access is off NY 28N, 3.9 mi N of the Olmstedville Rd./NY 28N intersection in Minerva and 2.8 mi S of the Hewitt Lake Club Rd. in Aiden Lair. A long curve in the road has an equally long pullout area on its E side. A DEC signpost marks the spot. ◀

THE WOODS ROAD wends its way up a slight grade, leveling at 0.1 mi. On a curve, at 0.3 mi, a side trail R leads to an open campsite. (From the campsite, a footpath descends 0.1 mi to the shore of Twentyninth Pond. The N half of the shoreline is state-owned.)

The trail continues up a minor grade. At 0.4 mi, the trail bears L and an old woods road ascends a hill R. From a height of land at 0.5 mi a long downgrade leads to a brook, which is crossed on corduroy at 0.8 mi. Still descending, the trail reaches the valley bottom at 1.0 mi where it crosses another brook immediately downstream from a high beaver dam on the N side of the trail.

The trail traverses one more minor hill line. Corduroy and minor rerouting at 1.8 mi mark the site of previous beaver activity. Then the final upgrade to Stony Pond commences, parallel to the S of Stony Pond Brook.

Stony Pond with its lean-to is reached at 2.1 mi. The lean-to sits at a slight elevation above the pond level. An open area offers a gentle breeze and many wildflowers. It's a beautiful location.

❋ Trail in winter: This is an excellent ski trail. Combined with the Stony Pond from Irishtown Trail (trail 59) and the ponds, an excellent day of backcountry skiing is available. The ponds are generally frozen by January, but care should always be taken when on ice.

🐾 Distances: To Twentyninth Pond side trail, 0.3 mi; to beaver dam on trail, 1.0 mi; to Stony Pond, 2.1 mi (3.4 km).

(59) Stony Pond from Irishtown Trail

Map: 17-J7

The hike from Irishtown makes a nice day trip. However, be prepared to gain 930 ft in elevation to the ridge beyond Little Sherman Pond on the way. A through trip from NY 28N, with vehicles at both ends of the trail, is a less difficult way to see this land.

▶ Trailhead: Access is off John Brannon Rd. in Irishtown. From the blinker light in Olmstedville, head N on the Minerva Rd. At 0.3 mi, at the Olmstedville village road sign, turn R. Travel 1.8 mi to Irishtown. Turn L at the ball field onto County Route 37, passing St. Mary's Church and cemetery. Pass the Minerva transfer station and then cross Minerva Stream bridge at 0.4 mi. Turn R at the John Brannon Rd. T intersection. Drive another 0.4 mi to the trailhead. A cable barrier at the W side of the road marks the location. There is room on the shoulder of the road to park. ◀

THE FIRST PART of the hike is over private land. Care should be taken to stay on the trail. The woods road heads N following red trail markers and yellow snowmobile trail markers. Avoid all side roads in this section.

At 0.2 mi the trail crosses Falls Brook. The remains of an old dam can be seen downstream. A large waterfall is downstream. Informal side trails lead to it; it is especially interesting in the springtime. Cascades of water pour down the brook on the L as elevation is gained.

At a fork at 0.3 mi, the trail continues straight over a knoll; the road L leads to a private camp. A Forest Preserve sign at 0.6 mi indicates that state land is being entered. Rushing water can be heard from deeper in the woods. The steady upgrade continues to 1.3 mi, where the trail steepens sharply for a short distance before moderating.

At a fork at 2.0 mi, a sign on a tree points the way to Sherman Pond. Bear R. An old woods road crosses the trail at 2.1 mi. Red tape to the R marks a snowmobile bypass of a muddy area.

A major trail jct. is reached at 2.5 mi. The red-marked foot trail to Stony Pond turns abruptly L and heads W. (The yellow-marked trail N is part of the original Stony Pond Trail, which once continued along the E side of Big Sherman Pond and crossed the neck between Big Sherman and Little Sherman Ponds until it was flooded by beaver activity. The first tenth of a mile is still used to provide snowmobile access to Big Sherman Pond, but the remainder of the old trail has disappeared.)

At 2.6 mi the trail crosses Falls Brook, the outlet of Big Sherman Pond, just below a beaver dam. (The trail from here to the end of Little Sherman Pond is overgrown in places. Note the location of the previous trail marker while scouting the next one.) The trail climbs away from the water, but returns twice before the end of Big Sherman Pond is reached at 3.1 mi. Here the beginning of the crossover trail (now flooded) is seen cutting back R to the shoreline.

The trail continues N and reaches Little Sherman Pond at 3.2 mi. A jct. is reached at the end of Little Sherman Pond. (The trail R once went to the E corner of Stony Pond and then NW to Center Pond; it no longer is used.) The trail turns L and climbs steeply to 3.4 mi. It then gradually descends, turning L above the shoreline as it approaches the S end of Stony Pond at 3.5 mi. (The yellow-marked trail directly to the shore provides snowmobile access to the pond.) At 3.8 mi, the trail crosses a brook in a small cove of the pond and bears R as it parallels a rock wall. The Stony Pond lean-to is at 3.9 mi. Here the trails from NY 28N and Hewitt Pond (trail 56) merge.

❈ Trail in winter: Refer to Stony Pond from NY 28N (trail 58, page 145).

🐾 Distances: To Forest Preserve land, 0.6 mi; to Stony Pond Trail jct., 2.5 mi; to Big Sherman Pond outlet, 2.6 mi; to Little Sherman Pond, 3.2 mi; to Stony Pond lean-to, 3.9 mi (6.3 km).

(60) **Blue Ledges Trail**

Map: J7

Blue Ledges is a unique place where the Hudson River makes a horseshoe bend at the base of gigantic cliffs. The trail to Blue Ledges is very pleasant to walk and the grades are relatively easy, except perhaps for the last few hundred yards down to the river.

The river run from below the Lake Abanakee dam on the Indian River through the Hudson River Gorge to North River is very popular among canoeists, kayakers, and private and commercial rafters (see ADK's *Canoe and Kayak Guide: East-Central New York State*). Commercial rafting on the river is heavy in the spring and fall when water is released from the dam on Lake Abanakee. Under the terms of an agreement between the Town of Indian Lake and DEC, there is a daily limit of 1000 people on commercial rafts. That many have been known to sweep by Blue Ledges on a spring Saturday.

▶ Trailhead: Access to the trailhead is from the North Woods Club Rd. off NY 28N, 1.7 mi N of the intersection of Minerva Lake Rd. and NY 28N in Minerva. The North Woods Club Rd. forks W near the height of land on a curve. (If approaching from the S on NY 28N, it is easy to drive by without noticing it.) The macadam strip soon becomes a narrow but generally smooth dirt road. The road crosses the Boreas

River 3.7 mi from NY 28N and shortly thereafter it crosses an abandoned railroad track as it winds and climbs steeply up a grade. After a descent, a large DEC signpost on the S side of the road marks the trailhead 6.7 mi from NY 28N. There is a large parking area on each side of the road. This road is plowed in winter, but it is advised that it not be used without 4WD and a taste for danger. ◀

THE BLUE-MARKED DEC trail immediately crosses an inlet brook of Huntley Pond on a bridge and heads S. At 0.1 mi, it reaches Huntley Pond. The trail follows the shoreline of this attractive pond for a short distance, then turns SW up a small grade. At a height of land the trail descends to a brook crossing at 0.6 mi.

Turning W, the trail parallels the stream, passing several sites of beaver activity. At 1.6 mi, the route moves away from the stream and gradually gains elevation. The trail swings around the end of a ridge and then heads SE. The roar of the Hudson River can be heard in the valley below, though one cannot see the river at this point.

A small rock lookout ledge is reached at 2.0 mi. In autumn, the view of the ridge across the river is beautiful here. The descent to the river now begins; gradual at first, but then moderate, the slope is not difficult.

The trail drops down more steeply at 2.4 mi and ends at the river's edge directly across from the Blue Ledges. The sheer cliffs rise over 300 ft into the sky. Rapids are downstream, but good swimming is upstream during low-water periods in summer.

This section of river is one of the finest paddling waters in the Northeast. It is evident that the commercial users of the river have been doing an excellent job keeping this area attractive.

If backpacking, please camp at least 150 ft away from the river. Collect and carry out all litter that accumulates during your stay.

❋ Trail in winter: The access route in summer is memorable enough to discourage most people from trying it in winter.

🐾 Distances: To Huntley Pond, 0.1 mi; to brook crossing after height of land, 0.6 mi; to lookout ledge, 2.0 mi; to Blue Ledges at Hudson River, 2.5 mi (4.0 km).

(61) **Rankin Pond Trail**

Map: 17

Rankin Pond is like any of hundreds of little ponds in the Adirondacks. It is, however, so easily accessible that it can be visited without using a whole day. Anyone with a few minutes to spare can take a pleasant respite from a road trip and have a relaxing interlude or lunch break.

▶ Trailhead: A DEC signpost (sometimes missing in early spring) marks the trailhead on the W side of NY 28N, 4.3 mi NW of Minerva and 4.3 mi S of the Boreas River bridge. There is parking for a few cars across the road from the trailhead. ◀

THE TRAIL FOLLOWS blue DEC trail markers and heads W from the parking area, parallel with the highway. It soon turns NW and a gradual descent into a hardwood forest commences. It crosses a small opening at 0.1 mi. Then a small climb up a rise must be achieved before Rankin Pond comes into view. A minor descent leads to the shore of the pond at 0.4 mi.

A small clearing presents an excellent view of the pond. A large rock makes a nice seat while the view of the water is enjoyed. There are yellow pond lilies, purple irises, and many other water flowers at this quiet spot in the wilderness.

✳ Trail in winter: This is a very short trail for winter use.

⚘ Distance: To Rankin Pond, 0.4 mi (0.6 km).

(62) **Linsey Marsh Trail**

Map: H7

Linsey Marsh is an elongated depression N of Hewitt Pond Mt. The trail travels over gradual grades on dry ground through a mixed-wood forest.

▶ Trailhead: The trailhead is off the E side of NY 28N, 1.1 mi S of the Boreas River bridge. A small DEC signpost marks the spot. ◀

THE TRAIL FOLLOWS yellow markers up a bank from the road. The direction changes from NE to N at 0.3 mi. After a height of land at 0.5 mi, there is a short jog E at 0.8 mi, but the general direction is NNE.

The trail crosses a brook on a dilapidated bridge at 1.1 mi. Then, a moderate grade between close trees climbs 100 ft and gradual grades again are the norm. The route swings E at 1.2 mi. Slightly rolling terrain continues to 1.4 mi, where the route again heads N. A long, gradual downhill slope to Linsey Marsh begins here.

Linsey Marsh is reached at 2.0 mi. It is impossible to get near the water, but the marsh is very interesting. Open water in its center is bordered by marsh grasses and flowers.

❋ Trail in winter: This is a little-used but quite pleasant trail for both snowshoers and skiers.

🕊 Distances: To height of land, 0.5 mi; to bridge over creek, 1.1 mi; to Linsey Marsh, 2.0 mi (3.2 km).

(63) Boreas River Trail

Map: H7

The Boreas River was alive with French-Canadian river runners every spring a hundred years ago. More than one lumberjack lost his life getting the logs down to the chain boom on the Hudson River at Glens Falls. Today, a footpath provides a beautiful little walk into Hewitt Eddy. If two vehicles are available, a 2.0 mi loop hike can be done by combining this walk with the Hewitt Eddy Trail (trail 64). The preferable direction for walking is from the Hewitt Eddy Trail to the Boreas River bridge.

▶ Trailhead: Access is on the W side of NY 28N, at the S end of the Boreas River bridge. This is 8.7 mi N of Minerva and 5.2 mi S of the NY 28N/Tahawus Rd. intersection. (The remains of an old public campsite are evident on the old bridge road, across the road from the trail. It has several open campsites, fireplaces, and picnic tables.) Parking is available on the old bridge road opposite the trail. ◀

BLUE DEC TRAIL MARKERS indicate the route along the E bank of the river. Attractive conifers and vibrant water sounds keep your interest. The trail stays close to the water, crossing occasional tributaries. Hewitt Eddy, a wide spot in the Boreas River, is at 1.2 mi. Here, a wide, placid pool circles on itself below the turbulent waters upstream—an interesting contrast.

The trail continues from this spot as the Hewitt Eddy Trail (trail 64). It continues for another 0.8 mi to NY 28N, 0.8 mi S of the Boreas River bridge.

❋ Trail in winter: This trail is not suitable for skiing.

🕊 Distances: To Hewitt Eddy, 1.2 mi (1.9 km). To NY 28N via Hewitt Eddy Trail, 2.0 mi (3.2 km).

(64) Hewitt Eddy Trail

Map: H7

The Hewitt Eddy Trail is an especially nice woods walk to the Boreas River. The variety of ferns, flowers, and trees is intriguing. The trail can be combined with the Boreas River Trail (trail 63) to make a through-trip of 2.0 mi total distance.

▶ Trailhead: Access to the trailhead is off the W side of NY 28N, 0.8 mi S of the Boreas River bridge. A small DEC sign marks the trailhead. ◀

THE TRAIL, with blue DEC trail markers, proceeds SW down a small grade. Soon it heads W up a short, steep rise. The rest of the trip is gradually downhill to the Boreas River. The route continues W, coming along the R side of Stony Pond Brook at 0.5 mi.

Drifting away from the brook, the trail heads N on level ground. It reaches Hewitt Eddy, a wide point in the Boreas River, at 0.8 mi. Here, rock forces the Boreas to split its flow. The eddy is where the waters rejoin in a long, lazy arc.

Upstream from the eddy, the trail is the Boreas River Trail (trail 63). It continues 1.2 mi along the E bank of the river to the Boreas River bridge. This is 0.8 mi N along NY 28N from the Hewitt Eddy trailhead.

❄ Trail in winter: The trail is suitable for snowshoeing, but not particularly interesting in winter.

⚹ Distances: To uphill grade, 0.2 mi; to Stony Pond Brook, 0.5 mi; to Hewitt Eddy, 0.8 mi (1.3 km). To NY 28N via Boreas River Trail, 2.0 mi (3.2 km).

(65) Vanderwhacker Mt. Trail

Maps: Page 153 and H7

The summit of Vanderwhacker Mt. provides perhaps the finest panorama of the High Peaks to be seen from the southern Adirondacks. Although no longer maintained by DEC, its fire tower is in good condition.

▶ Trailhead: Access to the trailhead is on a gravel road off the W side of NY 28N, immediately N of the Boreas River bridge. There is a signpost at the jct. The initial grade from the highway is on loose hardscrabble stone, but the road is satisfactory beyond this point if speed is controlled. Avoid a L turn at 1.5 mi just before crossing Vanderwhacker Brook on a bridge. Several open campsites and fireplaces are found in

The High Peaks from Vanderwhacker Mountain
PHOTOGRAPH BY RICHARD NOWICKI

this area. The road crosses abandoned railroad tracks and narrows noticeably. It comes to a jct. at 2.6 mi; the Vanderwhacker Mt. route bears R, whereas continuing past this jct. leads to the private Moose Pond Club, which is not open to the public. A small sign indicating the trailhead direction may be seen. The trailhead and parking area are soon reached (0.0 mi). ◄

THE WIDE TRAIL, with red DEC hiking trail and snowmobile trail markers, climbs gradually NW through a hardwood forest. Soon leveling off, it swings N along the L bank of a brook, which it crosses on a wide bridge at 0.3 mi.

A beaver dam on the R at 0.6 mi has flooded the trail, forcing its relocation to the L. A long marsh is on the L at 0.7 mi, with Little Beaver Mt. in the distant W. The hiking trail weaves in and out of the snowmobile trail as it follows the edge of the marsh. At 0.9 mi, a second beaver dam can be seen to the L and the trail begins to climb away from the marsh.

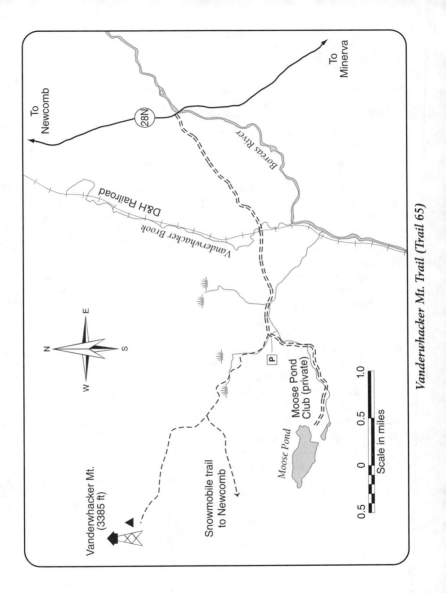

Vanderwhacker Mt. Trail (Trail 65)

The snowmobile trail turns L at 1.3 mi, bearing around the base of the mountain, while the hiking trail continues straight ahead. The grade becomes moderate just before the fire observer's cabin at 1.4 mi. The trail climbs up, through a large opening with grass and berry bushes, to the cabin and outbuildings.

The trail continues uphill between the buildings, the slope becoming moderate and then steep. At 1.8 mi, the grade eases appreciably as the trail passes through a small hollow. The remaining distance to the summit at 2.7 mi is extremely attractive with gradual upgrades.

The summit is closed in on three sides, but magnificent open views can be obtained to the N. Algonquin and Avalanche Pass stand out. Colden, Redfield, Marcy, Haystack, Allen, Gothics, Sawteeth, Nipple Top, Dix, and Macomb, as well as the Boreas Range and many minor peaks, can be seen. A 360° view is gained from the fire tower. Moose Pond is below to the S. Beaver Ponds and Split Rock Pond are more distant in the SW.

❋ Trail in winter: The access road is not plowed in winter and is excellent for skiing to the caretaker cabin. The skier can then switch to snowshoes and continue on to the summit.

🐾 Distances: To marsh, 0.7 mi; to fire observer's cabin, 1.4 mi; to end of steep slope, 1.8 mi; to summit, 2.7 mi (4.4 km). Ascent, 1650 ft (503 m). Elevation, 3385 ft (1032 m).

(66) Santanoni Preserve

Map: Page 155

The extensive trails of the Santanoni Preserve are described in ADK's Guide to Adirondack Trails: High Peaks Region. They provide many opportunities for day trips as well as southern access routes to the N-P Trail and the High Peaks. A brief introduction to this area is given here because those who come to the Newcomb area to do hikes described in this guide should know the Santanoni Preserve lies just to the N. The following has been taken from *Adirondack Trails: High Peaks Region*, edited by Tony Goodwin (slightly modified for use here).

This tract of land was transferred from private ownership to the State of New York in 1972 through the efforts of the Adirondack Conservancy. Most of this land is now part of the High Peaks Wilderness Area and provides a SE approach to the Cold River area.

This area has so far received very little use even though it offers

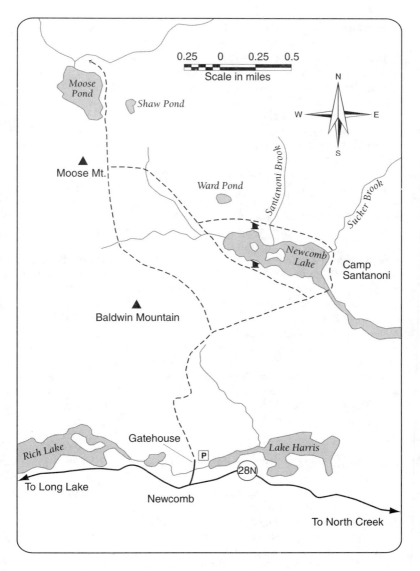

0.25 0 0.25 0.5
Scale in miles

N
W   E
S

Moose Pond

Shaw Pond

▲ Moose Mt.

Ward Pond

Santanoni Brook

Sucker Brook

Newcomb Lake

Camp Santanoni

▲ Baldwin Mountain

Gatehouse

Rich Lake

P

Lake Harris

28N

To Long Lake

Newcomb

To North Creek

Santanoni Preserve (Trail 66)

some outstanding opportunities for hiking, fishing, horseback riding, and skiing. The centerpiece of this area is 2.0 mi long Newcomb Lake, which has two lean-tos and many campsites along its pristine shores.

Remaining from the days of private ownership are two roads, leading to Newcomb Lake and Camp Santanoni (4.5 mi) and Moose Pond (6.7 mi), as well as a huge log structure—Camp Santanoni—on the NE shore of Newcomb Lake. The road to Newcomb Lake is still hard-packed and suitable for bicycles, and some people have used various wheeled carriers to transport boats to Newcomb Lake. No special camping permits are required, although the normal restrictions that apply to camping on any state land still apply here.

After years of debate as to whether or not the buildings could be maintained under the "forever wild" clause of the New York State Constitution, the issue was resolved in 2000 by reclassification of 32 acres of Vanderwhacker Wild Forest as the Camp Santanoni Historic Area. This reclassification allows the buildings to be restored and preserved, but motorized access, leasing, or commercial use of the property are prohibited. The National Park Service also designated Camp Santanoni a National Historic Landmark in 2000.

▶ Trailhead: Trails start from the gatehouse of the Santanoni Preserve. This is reached via a side road to the N, 0.3 mi W of the Newcomb Town Hall on NY 28N. A rustic Santanoni Preserve sign marks this side road. After crossing a narrow metal bridge and ascending a small hill past the gatehouse, you will find a dirt road to the R leading to large parking facilities and privies. The trailhead and trail register are on the entrance road past the side road to the parking area. ◀

✳ Trails in winter: The Santanoni Preserve trails are excellent and have dependable snow all winter.

Newcomb Visitor Interpretive Center

Map: Page 158

Many people, even those who have spent much time in the Adirondacks, know little about the region. The heritage, ecology, and geology of the Adirondacks are fascinating. Such knowledge and many other things are the purpose of both the Newcomb and Paul Smiths Visitor Interpretive Centers (VIC). Developed by the Adirondack Park Agency, both centers provide exhibits, audiovisual presentations, computer-interfaced informational services, educational programs, and beautiful trails for everyone to use. The centers have a year-round program of classes and evening speakers.

▶ Trailhead: The Newcomb VIC is located 1.4 mi W of the Newcomb Town Hall on NY 28N. There is a signpost. ◀

THE NEWCOMB VIC has three walking trails with frequent vistas and educational sites where ecological information is provided or various plant and animal life are identified. The 0.6 mi Rich Lake Trail is rated as easy. It has several places to sit and enjoy the water. The moderate 1.0 mi Sucker Brook Trail takes you through ancient cedar groves, across wetlands on wide boardwalks, and to the site of a log dam. Finally, the 0.9 mi Peninsula Forest Primeval Trail is rated as challenging. It has cedar and hemlock stands and crosses a wetland via a pontoon bridge.

These trail ratings are set by the center and are intended for use by visitors who are not necessarily hikers. Experienced hikers would find all of these trails easy or moderate in difficulty. Distances are as listed on the center's trail map. However, the Peninsula Trail begins part way along the Rich Lake Trail. If measured as a distinct round trip originating and ending at the VIC, the total distance for the Peninsula Trail would be 1.8 mi.

A fine day can be had by climbing Goodnow Mt. in the morning and then having lunch at the VIC before taking a walk around these trails and visiting the main building at the center.

❋ Trails in winter: These trails are suitable for snowshoeing, but are not designed for skiing.

(67) Goodnow Mt.

Map: Page 158

(A description of this trail can also be found in ADK's *Adirondack Trails: High Peaks Region.*)

The summit of Goodnow Mt. offers a very fine panorama of the High Peaks to the north. Mountain and trail are at the Archer and Anna Huntington Wildlife Forest Station, which is part of the College of Environmental Science and Forestry at Syracuse University. The forestry students maintain the trail and fire tower. This is an ideal trail for children and can be combined with a Newcomb Visitor Interpretive Center (VIC) visit. In the summer of 1993 the first part of

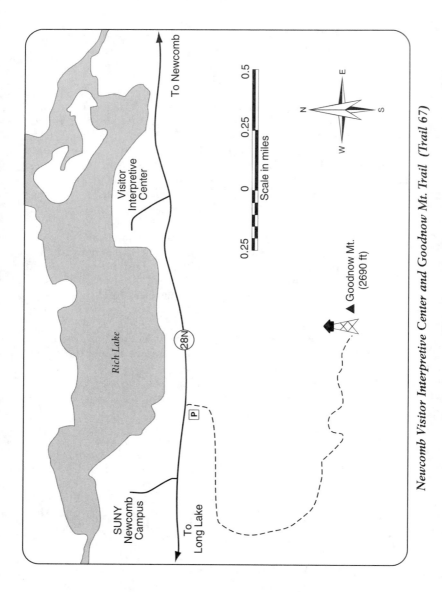

Newcomb Visitor Interpretive Center and Goodnow Mt. Trail (Trail 67)

the trail was rerouted, benches were added for resting along the way, and interpretive pamphlets were provided for hikers.

▶ Trailhead: Access to the trailhead is on the S side of NY 28N, 1.5 mi W of the entrance to the VIC near Newcomb. This point is also 11.6 mi E of Long Lake village. A large white sign marks the parking area. ◀

THE TRAIL LEAVES the parking area and trail register, marked by red trail markers with black arrows. It climbs moderately for about 200 yd, before swinging R. It traverses small rises and dips as it passes over a shelf, parallel to the highway. Maples, birches, and other hardwoods make up the forest growth.

A bridge spans a small brook at 0.5 mi and the trail then turns L. Moderate climbing starts at 0.7 mi. Steady elevation gain continues until the old trail, a woods road, is reached on the ridge crest at 0.9 mi. Bearing sharply L, as the forest growth opens up, the old woods road winds its way up the ridge. The road climbs gradually to 1.1 mi. It then ascends a moderate slope, leveling just before passing a concrete platform R at 1.4 mi. A side trail R in a notch at 1.5 mi leads to a charming covered well. Then a small horse barn is passed R.

The trail becomes a rocky path and steepens. Spruce and balsam fir close in. Open rock at 1.8 mi provides a view to the R. Then, after a drop down briefly into a small depression, a long gradual incline leads to the rocky summit at 1.9 mi.

One can see 23 major peaks from the summit fire tower. The Santanoni Range is close in at the NW; Marcy and Algonquin stand out in the N; Vanderwhacker Mt. with its tower is in view to the E.

❄ Trail in winter: This is an excellent snowshoe outing mountain. Measure your mileage from town carefully. High banks may make trail location difficult.

🐾 Distances: To bridge, 0.5 mi; to merger with old trail, 0.9 mi; to covered well, 1.5 mi; to summit, 1.9 mi (3.1 km). Ascent, 1040 ft (317 m). Elevation, 2690 ft (820 m). ◆

RICHARD NOWICKI

Northeast Section

The trails of the Northeast Section are accessible from I-87 (Adirondack Northway). In the heyday of Adirondack hotels, the Schroon Lake area was a transportation crossroads. Summer people would take a stagecoach from Crown Point at Lake Champlain and head west. After a night at Root's Hotel, they might go on to Rufus Fiske's Lakeside Inn at Clear Pond, John Moore's hotel at Mud Lake (Elk Lake), or perhaps the Tahawus Club near Newcomb. It was a slower paced lifestyle, but the same mountains, ponds, and streams were enjoyed then as are enjoyed by today's hikers. Many of the bridle paths and carriage roads developed for those hotel guests are now the trails described in this guide.

One point of interest for travelers in this area is Balance Rock, a 12 ft diameter circular boulder perched on a second large slanting boulder. Why it doesn't roll off its sloping base is a curiosity. Balance Rock is located on the N side of Blue Ridge Rd. 8.3 mi N and then E of the intersection of NY 28N and Tahawus Rd. in Newcomb and 6.2 mi W of the Elk Lake Rd.

Recommended trails in this section include:

SHORT HIKES:
- Bailey Pond: 2.0 mi (3.2 km) round trip. An easy walk to a pretty pond.
- Roosevelt Truck Trail: 5.0 mi (8.1 km) round trip. A hike through coniferous forests.

MODERATE HIKES:
- Mt. Severance: 2.4 mi (3.9 km) round trip. A climb up a small mountain for nice views of Schroon Lake and Paradox Lake.
- Cheney Pond and Lester Flow: 5.2 mi (8.4 km) round trip. A beautiful view awaits those who hike to the old dam site at the flow.

HARDER HIKES:

◆ Hoffman Notch: 14.8 mi (23.9 km) round trip. A long hike through exquisite wilderness.

TRAIL DESCRIBED	TOTAL MILES (one way)	PAGE
Hoffman Notch	7.4 (11.9 km)	162
Bailey Pond	1.0 (1.6 km)	164
Mt. Severance	1.2 (1.9 km)	166
Cheney Pond and Lester Flow	2.6 (4.2 km)	168
Roosevelt Truck Trail	2.5 (4.0 km)	170

(68) Hoffman Notch Trail

Map: Page 165

The Hoffman Notch Trail is a wilderness walk through a magnificent forest of huge trees. The route today varies little from that shown on the 1908 *Adirondack Forest Map* of the Forest, Fish, and Game Commission. The woods have been Forest Preserve land since that period of rampant forest fires, and it is quite likely that the area is wilder now than it was then. Certainly, there are fewer visitors now than in the earlier time of hotels and guides. For all the wildness, the walking is rather gentle, particularly on the southern side of the notch. Those planning a point-to-point hike will need a car at each trailhead. The trail is described from S to N.

▶ Trailheads: Trail access from the N end of the notch is off the S side of Blue Ridge Rd., approximately 5.7 mi W of Exit 29 of I-87. This is 1.4 mi beyond the Elk Lake Rd. sign and immediately past the bridge over The Branch stream. If approaching from Newcomb on Blue Ridge Rd., it is 13.1 mi from the intersection of NY 28N and the Tahawus Rd. The trailhead has no sign, but has a green metal signpost and a small sandy pullout. The trail drops down a small grade.

The S trailhead is at Loch Muller. Turn W off NY 9 onto Hoffman Rd. in the village of Schroon Lake. Drive 6.4 mi to the jct. of Loch Muller Rd. Turn R. Continue 2.4 mi to an old white hotel building above Warrens Pond with a delightful sign commemorating a tall tree at the road's edge. From this point onward the dirt road narrows. After 0.1 mi turn R at a fork and proceed another 0.1 mi to a large turnabout where the trailhead is located. A DEC trail sign marks the trailhead (0.0 mi). ◀

THE TRAIL HEADS generally NE following yellow trail markers down a gradual slope. It crosses the W branch of Trout Brook (Bailey Pond Outlet) on a bridge at 0.4 mi. The trail now gradually ascends, trending ENE from 0.8 mi. It reaches the N branch of Trout Brook at 1.2 mi, abruptly veers to the N, and comes to a jct. (The blue-marked trail R crosses the N branch and heads SE to Big Pond and then out to Hoffman Rd. It should not be attempted, as long stretches are overgrown.) Continue straight. The level course generally follows the N branch's W bank, sometimes close by and farther away at times.

The first of many large glacial erratics appears at 1.6 mi in a lush fern meadow. Then, at 2.0 mi, the trail clings to the W bank of the stream for quite some time, creating a musical interlude amidst the beauty of nature.

Glimpses of a large beaver marsh can be seen through the trees to the E at 2.7 mi. The trail is overgrown in places from here to Big Marsh. Watch for the yellow trail markers.

The trail comes to the W shore of Big Marsh at 3.8 mi. Excellent views of Texas Ridge, Hoffman Mt., and Blue Ridge Mt. are found here. Big Marsh is actually a very pretty large pond that makes an ideal lunch spot.

Returning to open woods, the trail makes an abrupt R at 4.0 mi. The grade is so moderate you may be through the notch and not realize it until you notice that the trail is following the R bank of a tributary stream downstream.

The trail becomes a wide old wagon route. At a jct. at 4.4 mi, avoid the L turn, which crosses the stream. At 4.6 mi the rushing sounds of water indicate Hoffman Notch Brook. Rock-hop across. (This idyllic spot is worthy of exploration. Hike the short distance upstream around the bend to see the cascading waters cutting through ancient rock. Indistinct anglers' paths lead up to the small pond at the entrance to Hornet Notch. Hoffman Notch Brook makes a good bushwhack route to Hoffman Mt. and the Blue Ridge.)

From this spot to Blue Ridge Rd. the trail descends 500 ft. The valley closes perceptibly, creating an air of eerie wildness. The stream must again be rock-hopped to the L bank at 4.8 mi.

At 5.0 mi the alert hiker will note splendid high cliffs about 100 yd L of the trail. Here, remnants of a glacial meltwater overflow standout. Even today, spring snowmelts pour over this opening in Washburn Ridge, creating an awesome display of nature's power. Water falls nearly 200 ft to the base of the cliffs.

The route continues its descent amidst rugged boulders that give evidence of a violent past. At 5.8 mi, the chassis of an old Army half-track sits beside the trail, which recrosses Hoffman Notch Brook to the R bank at 6.0 mi. At 6.3 mi, the trail passes under power lines. (USGS maps show the trail heading E near here and then turning N through a marshy area. By owner permission, the trail has been relocated through posted property. Please stay on the trail and do not camp in this section.) Continue N.

Hoffman Notch Brook is recrossed yet again on a wide bridge at 6.5 mi, followed by a crossing of Sand Pond Brook on another wide bridge at 6.6 mi. Four small bridges cross low areas and streams in the next three-tenths of a mile and the trail turns E up a gradual slope. Traffic on the Blue Ridge Rd. may be heard.

At 7.1 mi, the trail passes through a large grove of white cedar, and at 7.3 mi it turns L on a woods road. A side path leads around a barrier gate at 7.4 mi, and then a roadway leads up a short grade to the trailhead on Blue Ridge Rd.

❄ Trail in winter: This is an excellent snowshoe or backwoods skiing trail. Through trips are possible in winter. The N side of the notch requires good control.

🐾 Distances: To W branch of Trout Brook, 0.4 mi; to N branch of Trout Brook, 1.2 mi; to Big Marsh, 3.8 mi; to Hoffman Notch Brook, 4.6 mi; to Washburn Ridge cliffs, 5.0 mi; to Sand Pond Brook, 6.6 mi; to Blue Ridge Rd., 7.4 mi. (11.9 km).

(69) Bailey Pond Trail

Map: Page 165

Bailey Pond is a pretty little body of water that makes a good destination for a short walk. The trip can be extended to make a full day's outing.

▶ Trailhead: Access to the trailhead is the same as for the S trailhead for the Hoffman Notch Trail (trail 68). ◀

THE TRAIL LEAVES the rear of the parking area, following blue DEC trail markers to the NW. Passing behind a camp, it joins a woods road at 0.1 mi and continues with minor grades to 0.9 mi, where a side trail L, just before the outlet of Bailey Pond (W branch of Trout Brook), leads 0.1 mi W to Bailey Pond. There are a few rocks along the shore; they make pleasant places to sit and observe the water.

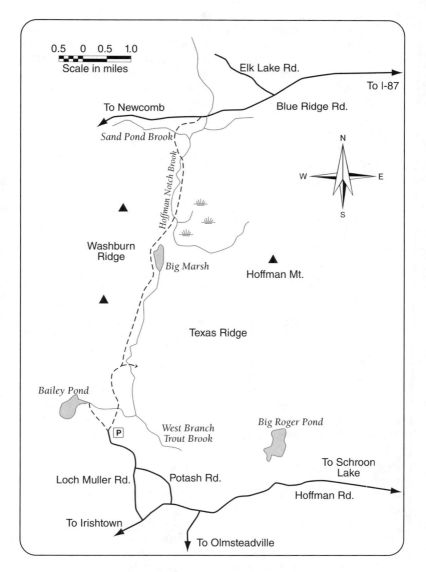

Hoffman Notch and Bailey Pond Trails (Trails 68, 69)

The hike can be extended for an enjoyable walk through open woods. The woods road continues as an unmarked trail beyond the outlet. Broad and easy to follow for the next mile beyond the outlet, it generally parallels Bailey Pond Inlet, which comes out of the pass between Bailey Hill and Washburn Ridge. The route once turned L at 2.0 mi and wound up the ridge to the summit of Bailey Hill. However, this section of the road has become overgrown and any attempt to climb the hill must be considered a bushwhack.

❄ Trail in winter: This is a little-used but relatively easy trail for skiing.

🦌 Distances: To woods road, 0.2 mi; to Bailey Pond outlet, 0.9 mi; to Bailey Pond, 1.0 mi. (1.6 km).

(70) Mt. Severance Trail

Map: Page 167

Tectonic geologists tell us the Adirondack Mountains are currently growing at a rate exceeding that of the Himalayas. The 1953 edition of the Schroon Lake 15-min. USGS quadrangle map shows a Severance Hill. However, by 1984, the large DEC sign along US 9 indicated the trailhead for Mt. Severance. Whether this can be taken as sound scientific evidence of great vertical growth in only 31 years is highly speculative. Nevertheless, it can be said in all sincerity that a climb up Mt. Severance distinctly offers more the feel of a mountain than of a hill. This little mountain rises 750 ft above the parking area to an elevation of 1638 ft.

▶ Trailhead: Access is off US 9, 1.9 mi N of the village of Schroon Lake. If approaching on I-87, use Exit 28 and head E a short distance to US 9. Turn R and drive S, 0.6 mi to a large DEC signpost on the W side of the road. A large split-level parking area is provided. ◀

THE YELLOW-MARKED DEC trail leaves the R rear of the parking area. It immediately passes under both lanes of I-87 through large culverts constructed for hiker use. Bearing L, the trail climbs a small rise to level ground.

The next 0.2 mi is an easy walk through pleasant woods. Then, following a brief climb, the trail crosses a stream on a bridge at 0.3 mi. Turning L and then R, the grade steepens. The remainder of the trip is a series of moderate grades interspersed with welcome level stretches.

After a second bridge, at 0.8 mi, the trail passes through a magnifi-

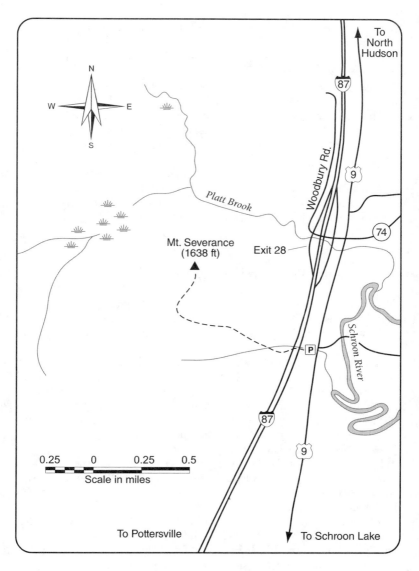

Mt. Severance Trail (Trail 70)

cent stand of large hemlock. One can't help but admire the beauty of such trees.

At 0.9 mi, the trail becomes moderately steep. First swinging L, it then turns R and heads for the summit. The first good view is from a clearing facing SE at 1.1 mi. The N end of Schroon Lake stands out before you. Pharaoh Mt. can be seen in the distance behind the lake.

The trail continues N to 1.2 mi and another clearing. Good views of Paradox Lake can be seen to the NE. The trail doesn't actually reach the summit, which is an easy short bushwhack to the W through open deciduous woods.

❄ Trail in winter: Though a snowmobile trail in the winter, this trail is better suited for an excellent snowshoe outing.

🐾 Distances: To hemlock stand, 0.8 mi; to first lookout, 1.1 mi; to second lookout, 1.2 mi (1.9 km). Ascent, 713 ft (217 m). Elevation, 1638 ft (499 m).

(71) Cheney Pond and Lester Flow

Map: G7

The walk to Lester Flow is along an almost level grassy woods road. It makes a pleasant day hike or a fine introductory backpacker route. The view of the Great Range up Lester Flow from the Lester Flow dam site is unusually good.

A dam at the S End of Lester Flow made the extensive waterway connecting Lester Flow and Cheney Pond, which is shown on USGS topographic maps. However, the dam washed out and Lester Flow is much lower and smaller than the maps make it appear. (Paddlers find it difficult to pass from Cheney Pond into Lester Flow.) Except in periods of very low water levels, it is difficult to cross the outlet of Lester Flow below the dam site. If this can be done, it is possible to follow an old trail E and then N 0.9 mi to its intersection with the Irishtown snowmobile trail. One could then hike another 8.0 mi to Irishtown, but the way is often wet, and it is not as pleasant hiking in summer as it is skiing in winter.

▶ Trailhead: Access is from the Blue Ridge Rd., 5.3 mi N and then E from the intersection of NY 28N and the Tahawus Rd. in Newcomb and 9.2 mi W of the Elk Lake Rd. A DEC signpost and parking area mark the location on the S side of Blue Ridge Rd. ◀

THE TRAIL HEADS S on a hardscrabble road, gradually descending to

0.4 mi, where it turns R into what at first appears to be an informal campsite. (The hardscrabble road continues straight ahead 0.2 mi to Cheney Pond. There is a turnaround and picnic table at the water's edge. While it is possible to drive a vehicle this far, it is not recommended unless you have a boat to carry.)

The trail continues through a small clearing and soon reaches a barrier, prohibiting further vehicular travel. The road becomes a grassy lane and trends principally S. For the most part the way is level. Grades, when they occur, are minor.

Lester Flow.
PHOTOGRAPH BY BRUCE C. WADSWORTH

Red DEC snowmobile markers are occasional.

The trail makes a short jog to the W at 0.8 mi and then resumes its way to the S. There are tamaracks, cedar, balsam fir, and red spruce. The route winds a bit from 1.8 to 1.9 mi. Thereafter, a raised bank is on the L of the trail.

A long gradual downgrade leads to an extensive beaver dam bordering the R edge of the trail at 2.4 mi. Turn L at a jct. at 2.5 mi. This leads to an open campsite with a fire ring. A path leads 40 ft to the shore of Lester Flow at 2.6 mi, just above the dam site.

Up Lester Flow in the distant NNW, the Great Range in the High Peaks can be seen. The bare rock faces of Basin and Gothics are prominent. Downstream, the remains of the large crib dam site are interesting.

❄ Trail in winter: This is an excellent ski trail in a region of dependable snow. Skiers often make a loop trip by skiing up the flow to the Cheney Pond turnaround point. Be sure to test ice thickness carefully before setting out on the flow.

🐾 Distances: To Cheney Pond jct., 0.4 mi; to beaver dam, 2.4 mi; to Lester Flow, 2.6 mi (4.2 km).

Roosevelt Truck Trail (unmaintained)

Map: G7

An old state truck trail off Blue Ridge Rd. makes a beautiful place for a walk through a spruce and balsam fir forest. The wide grassy lane cuts through woods that cling to the road's edges. A point-to-point trip will require two cars.

▶ Trailhead: Access to the S trailhead is off NY 28N, 0.3 mi S of the railroad tracks and 1.6 mi N of the Boreas River bridge. A narrow paved road runs SE off the E side of NY 28N. There is a barrier at the trailhead on the L side of this road 0.1 mi from the highway. (The road dead-ends a short distance past the trailhead at an open campsite. No water is at this location.) ◀

ACCESS TO THE N trailhead is off the S side of Blue Ridge Rd. 4.0 mi N and then E of the intersection of NY 28N and the Tahawus Rd. in Newcomb and 10.5 mi W of the Elk Lake Rd. Since the trailhead is on the outside bank of a curve, care must be taken to spot it. There is a barrier gate with low stone walls on each side at the trailhead.

From the N trailhead, the wide unmarked road is a grassy lane heading S down a small grade. Then, after a minor rise at 0.2 mi, a 150 ft moderate descent ends at 0.5 mi, where the trail crosses a tributary of Vanderwhacker Brook on a wide bridge. The gradual upgrade away from the brook heads SW, but turns S again at 1.0 mi. Minor grades then give some variation in the trail.

A small section of deciduous trees occurs at 1.6 mi. The route turns SW again at 1.9 mi and then S, W, and SW in its last half-mile. A long, very gradual downgrade passes rocky boulders at trailside. A barrier gate, hidden from the paved road in the high summer grass, marks the S trailhead at 2.5 mi.

❄ Trail in winter: This is a good ski trail, though sometimes hard to locate at its N end.

🐾 Distances: To tributary bridge, 0.5 mi; to deciduous trees, 1.6 mi; to S trailhead, 2.5 mi (4.0 km). ◆

Southeast Section

There is little state-owned land in the Southeast Section. Consequently, there are few hiking trails. However, those that do exist are very nice. They offer a walk along the Hudson River, visits to two ponds, and a walk through an ancient hemlock forest.

SHORT HIKES:
- Charles Lathrop Pack Demonstration Forest Nature Trail: 2.2 mi (3.5 km) round trip. A walk through a forest of huge hemlocks and ferns to the tallest white pine in the state.
- Hudson River Recreation Area: A number of loop trails next to the Hudson River offer a variety of short walks.

MODERATE HIKE:
- Palmer Pond: 2.0 mi (3.2 km) round trip. A hike along an old woods road to a large pond.

TRAIL DESCRIBED	TOTAL MILES (one way)	PAGE
Charles Lathrop Pack Demonstration		
Forest Nature Trail	0.1 (0.2 km)	171
Hudson River Recreation Area		174
Palmer Pond	1.0 (1.6 km)	174

(72) Charles Lathrop Pack Demonstration Forest Nature Trail

Map: Page 172

This disabled-accessible nature trail is maintained by the State University of New York College of Environmental Science and Forestry. It offers a very appealing walk of a little over a mile through one of the greatest assemblages of truly huge hemlock trees in the Adirondacks. Its most striking attraction, however, is Grandmother's Tree. Grandmother's Tree is at least 315 years old and, with a height of approximately 175 ft, is the tallest white pine tree on record in the state.

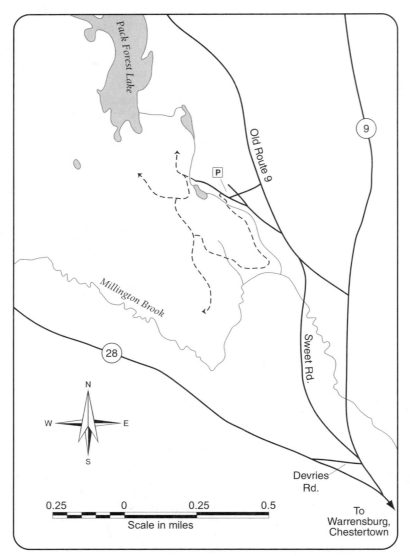

Charles Lathrop Pack Demonstration Forest Nature Trail
(Trail 72)

▶ Trailhead: Access is off the W side of US 9, 0.7 mi N of the US 9 and NY 28 intersection N of Warrensburg. A large sign marks the spot. Turn onto the macadam road and follow the directional signs for the nature trail parking lot. At 0.6 mi., a sign points R to parking in an unpaved open area. Returning to the main road, turn R and walk 150 yd along the road until you see the sign at L labeled "Grandmother's Tree Nature Trail." Printed trail guides are available at the trailhead. ◀

THE TRAIL ENTERS an oak and hemlock forest from the trailhead (0.0 mi). It crosses a gurgling brook on a bridge at 150 ft and the valley widens. White pine and yellow birch are now found. The trail gradually circles a glacial hill on the R. Various ferns, mosses, and lycopodia

Birch in the Moose River Plains
PHOTOGRAPH BY RICHARD NOWICKI

keep your interest, as the trail swings N among huge hemlocks.

The trail crosses two more bridges at 0.4 mi and 0.5 mi before reaching Grandmother's Tree, with its top soaring out of sight in the forest canopy, at 0.6 mi. Less than 50 yd from the tree, the trail passes the last interpretive marker and turns R on a woods road. It turns R again at a T intersection at 0.8 mi. The winding dirt road then skirts a small pond with lily pads to a third R turn at 0.9 mi. Passing through a set of buildings on a paved road, the trail ends at the parking lot on the L at 1.1 mi.

❊ Trail in winter: This trail is very short for a winter trip, but several of the roads in this facility can be walked or skied in winter.

🐾 Distances: To Grandmother's Tree, 0.6 mi; to T intersection, 0.8 mi; to parking lot, 1.1 mi (1.8 km).

(73) Hudson River Recreation Area

Map: Page 175

A joint venture of DEC and Warren County, the Hudson River Recreation Area provides canoe access to the Hudson River, a picnic area, hiking trails, and snowshoeing and cross-country skiing trails. Users can enjoy a stay of a few hours or a day in an attractive setting of towering pines adjacent to the Hudson River.

▶ Trailhead: Access to the trailhead is off the W side of Hudson St., 2.5 mi NW of the Floyd Bennett Park stoplight in Warrensburg. The N end of Hudson St. intersects NY 28, 1.7 mi N of the NY 28 and US 9 intersection. The nature trail is 2.2 mi S from NY 28. A large nature trail and canoe access sign points the way to a parking area. There is a large wooden map at the trailhead; printed trail guides were once available, but have not been for several years. The trail once had interpretive signs along it, but many of these have disappeared and not been replaced. ◀

THE MAP AT THE TRAILHEAD displays a number of interconnected trails that can be combined in a variety of loops ranging from 0.2 mi to 1.0 mi. The trail heading straight (W) from the trailhead reaches the Hudson River in 0.2 mi. Although most of the trails are easy to hike, a couple of short, moderate to steep pitches are encountered on the outermost loop (marked yellow on the trailhead map). The northernmost red loop (on the far R on the trailhead map) can be used to access the

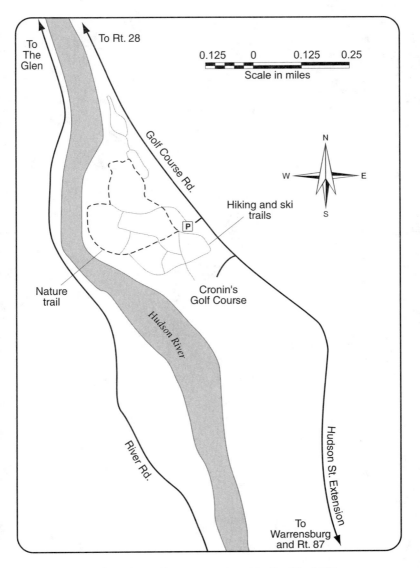

Hudson River Recreation Area Trails (Trail 73)

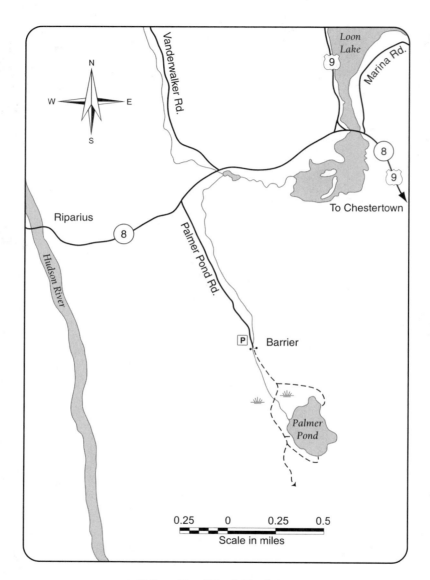

Palmer Pond Trail (Trail 74)

Hudson River, but the loop itself is overgrown (2001).

❊ Trail in winter: Many cross-country trails, some requiring considerable skill, weave through this area. While none are very long, when combined they provide a nice circuit.

(74) Palmer Pond Trail

Map: Page 176

Palmer Pond is a large pond that can be reached by an easy walk along a woods road. Side trails provide a variety of attractive vistas.

▶ Trailhead: Access to the trailhead is at the end of Palmer Pond Rd., off NY 8. Palmer Pond Rd. is 1.0 mi E of the Hudson River at Riparius and 1.0 mi W of the intersection of NY 8 and US 9, W of Chestertown. A barrier gate at 0.8 mi blocks Palmer Pond Rd. Parking is available for several vehicles at the barrier gate; additional parking spots can be found in the woods before the gate. ◀

FROM THE TRAILHEAD at the barrier gate (0.0 mi), a woods road heads S. After passing a flooded area on the R at 0.1 mi, the road ascends a minor knoll. At a jct. just over the crest of the knoll at 0.3 mi, continue straight. (The wide trail L makes a nice side trip. It skirts a marshy cove and reaches the E shore of the pond 0.4 mi from the road.)

The trail levels at a 150 ft beaver dam at 0.4 mi. This very large dam has totally flooded a small valley. Avoid the side trail L at the beginning of the dam. Continue on, across the solid, wide dam.

The road then ascends a gradual grade to Palmer Pond. Short side trails leading to the pond shore branch L at 0.5 mi and 0.6 mi. The road continues to a jct. in a clearing at 0.7 mi. Bear L. (The road straight ahead continues another 0.9 mi to private land. Although hikers must turn back at the boundary, the round trip offers a nice woods walk and occasional glimpses of old stone walls and foundations.) Skirting the pond, the trail terminates at a wide opening on its SW shore at 1.0 mi. The broad expanse of the pond can be seen from this vantage point. (The road continues beyond the opening, but the land is posted and should not be entered.)

❊ Trail in winter: These trails are suitable for skiing and snowshoeing, although they must be shared with snowmobilers.

🐾 Distances: To beaver dam, 0.4 mi; to clearing jct., 0.7 mi; to SW corner of pond, 1.0 mi (1.6 km). ◆

Appendix I

Glossary of Terms

Azimuth	A clockwise compass bearing swung from north.
Bivouac	Camping in the open with improvised shelter or no shelter.
Bushwhacking	Off-trail hiking, often with compass and map essential for direction.
Col	A pass between high points of a ridgeline.
Corduroy	Logs laid side by side across a trail to assist travel in wet areas.
Fire ring	A rough circle of stones used as a site in which to build small fires.
Lean-to	A three-sided shelter with an overhanging roof and one open side.
Logging road	A road used to haul logs after lumbering; often found in marshy areas which would be frozen in winter.
Summit	The top of a mountain.
Tote road	A woods road used year-round for hauling supplies; found on dry ground slopes.
Vlei	A low marshy area (pronounced "vly")

Appendix II

State Campgrounds in or near the Central Region

Campgrounds have been established by the DEC at many attractive spots throughout the state. Listed below are those campgrounds that might be useful as bases of operations for hiking in the Central Adirondacks region.

Information on state campgrounds and procedures for making reservations can be found on the Web at www.dec-campgrounds.com and in a brochure titled "Breathe In, Camp Out." This brochure is available at DEC regional offices; by telephoning the DEC Bureau of Recreation at 518-457-2500; or by writing to them at 625 Broadway, Albany, NY 12233-5253.

Indian Lake Islands. NY 30, 14.0 mi N of Speculator. Offers open camping on E shore of Indian Lake and on Indian Lake islands. Sites have privies and picnic tables. Sites can be reached only by boat.

Lake Durant. NY 28, 3.0 mi E of Blue Mt. Lake. Beautiful swimming area in full view of Blue Mt.

Lake Eaton. NY 30, 2.5 mi W of Long Lake.

Lewey Lake. NY 30, 14.0 mi N of Speculator.

Moffit Beach. NY 8, 4.0 mi W of Speculator.

Sacandaga. NY 30, 4.0 mi S of Wells. A campsite area along the W Branch of the Sacandaga River.

Eagle Point. US 9, 2.0 mi N of Pottersville.

Lake Harris. Off NY 28N, 3.0 mi N of Newcomb. This is a good base for many seldom-hiked trails.

Acknowledgments

Many people, from strangers met on the trail to friends and family, offer encouragement and assistance when they learn you are editing a guidebook.

Betty Lou Bailey, Terry Brosseau, Jack Freeman, Emily and Howard Hart, and David Trithart thoughtfully sent me trail updates. Don Greene was especially helpful in informing me about the Schaefer Trail on Gore Mountain. Fred Cady; Elsie, Alisa, and Shirley Cagle; Don Greene; Russ Guard; and David and Gregory Rubin accompanied me on hikes, providing companionship as well as keen observations. Russ in particular is to be commended for his scouting ability and insightful advice on some of the most obscure trails.

DEC personnel, including Mark Kralovic, forest ranger, Wells; Tad Norton, senior forester, Warrensburg DEC; Bruce Richards, conservation operations supervisor I, Northville DEC; and Edwin Russell, forest ranger, Schroon Lake, generously shared their knowledge on state property acquisitions and trail conditions. Karin Verschoor, mineral resource specialist, Geographic Information System Section, Albany DEC, was especially helpful on boundary issues. Whether it was during my visits to Northville or in our e-mail correspondence, Thomas V. Kapelewski, forester, Northville DEC, freely offered his time and expertise. His guidance on a host of matters, including property issues, trail conditions, maps, and contacts, was invaluable.

Patrick Arceri, formerly the unit forester for the Speculator Unit of International Paper Company, advised me on hiking and parking issues related to IP land, and took me on a tour of logging operations near Kunjamuk Cave.

It has been a pleasure to work with Neal Burdick, Forest Preserve Series editor, and ADK staff members Bill Brosseau, formerly acting publications director; John Kettlewell, publications director; Andrea Masters, publications editor; and Bonnie Langdon, publications coordinator. A more dedicated and professional group of people would be hard to find.

Many thanks to each of them and above all to my wife, Elsie, whose patience and wholehearted support sustained me through all the hours I spent in the field or on the computer.

About the Editors

LARRY CAGLE has a Ph.D. in sociology and was most recently Director of the Health Services Research and Special Studies Unit, New York State Department of Health. In addition to other work with the New York State Office of Mental Health, he was formerly a professor of sociology at Illinois Wesleyan University, Skidmore College, and Pennsylvania State University. He is the author of many professional publications, reports, and presentations.

NEAL BURDICK is a native of Plattsburgh, New York. He has hiked and canoed in the Adirondacks all his life. He began his association with ADK as a "hutboy" at Johns Brook Lodge more than thirty years ago, and he continues that relationship today as editor of ADK's Forest Preserve Series, The Adirondack Reader, and Adirondac magazine. He is a graduate of St. Lawrence University and is currently Associate Director of University Communications and University Editor there as well as a freelance writer.

Adirondack Mountain Club

ADKers choose from friendly outings, for those just getting started with local chapters, to Adirondack backpacks and international treks. Learn gradually through chapter outings or attend one of our schools, workshops, or other programs. A sampling includes:
- Alpine Flora
- Ice Climbing
- Rock Climbing
- Basic Canoeing/Kayaking
- Bicycle Touring
- Cross-country Skiing and Snowshoeing
- Mountain Photography
- Winter Mountaineering
- Birds of the Adirondacks
- Geology of the High Peaks ... and more!

For more information:
ADK Member Services Center
(Exit 21 off the Northway, I-87)
814 Goggins Road, Lake George, NY 12845-4117

ADK Heart Lake Program Center
P.O. Box 867, Lake Placid, NY 12946-0867

Information: 518-668-4447
Membership: 800-395-8080
Publications and merchandise: 800-395-8080
Education: 518-523-3441
Facilities' reservations: 518-523-3441
E-mail: adkinfo@adk.org
Web site: www.adk.org

Join Us

We are a nonprofit membership organization that brings together people with interests in recreation, conservation, and environmental education in the New York State Forest Preserve.

Membership Benefits

- **Discovery:**
  ADK can broaden your horizons by introducing you to new places, recreational activities, and interests

- **Enjoyment:**
  Being outdoors more and loving it more

- **People:**
  Meeting others and sharing the fun

- *Adirondac* **Magazine**

- **Member Discounts:**
  20% off on guidebooks, maps, and other ADK publications; discount on lodge stays; discount on educational programs

- **Satisfaction:**
  Knowing you're doing your part and that future generations will enjoy the wilderness as you do

- **Chapter Participation:**
  Brings you the fun of outings and other social activities and the reward of working on trails, conservation, and education projects at the local level. You can also join as a member at large. Either way, all Club activities and benefits are available.

Membership

To Join

Call **800-395-8080** (Mon.–Sat., 8:30 A.M.–5:00 P.M.), visit www.adk.org, or send this form with payment to:

Adirondack Mountain Club
814 Goggins Road
Lake George, NY 12845-4117

Check Membership Level:

o Individual	$45
o Family	$55*
o Student (full time, 18 and over)	$35
o Senior (65 or over)	$35
o Senior Family	$45*
o Individual Life	$1200
o Family Life	$1800*

School _____

*Includes associate/family members
Fees subject to change.

Name _____
Address _____
City _____ State _____ Zip _____
Home Telephone ( )_____

❏ I want to join as a Chapter member*
❏ I want to join as a member at large

List spouse and children under 18 with birth dates:

Spouse _____ _____
Child _____ Birth date _____
Child _____ Birth date _____

Bill my: ❏ MASTERCARD ❏ AMERICAN EXPRESS
❏ VISA   Exp. Date _____

_____
Signature (required for charge)

* For details, call **800-395-8080** (Mon.–Sat., 8:30 A.M.–5:00 P.M.)

ADK is a nonprofit, tax-exempt organization. Membership fees, excluding $10 for membership benefits, are tax deductible, to the extent allowed by law.

GCR

Adirondack ADK Mountain Club

List of Publications

The Adirondack Mountain Club, Inc.

814 Goggins Road, Lake George, NY 12845-4117
518-668-4447/Orders only: **800-395-8080** (Mon.–Sat., 8:30–5:00)
www.adk.org

BOOKS

Adirondack Canoe Waters: North Flow

Adirondack Mountain Club Canoe and Kayak Guide: East-Central New York State

Adirondack Mountain Club Canoe Guide to Western & Central New York State

An Adirondack Passage: The Cruise of the Canoe Sairy Gamp

An Adirondack Sampler I: Day Hikes for All Seasons

An Adirondack Sampler II: Backpacking Trips

Catskill Day Hikes for All Seasons

Climbing in the Adirondacks: A Guide to Rock & Ice Routes

Forests & Trees of the Adirondack High Peaks Region

Kids on the Trail! Hiking with Children in the Adirondacks

Our Wilderness: How the People of New York Found,
Changed, and Preserved the Adirondacks

Ski and Snowshoe Trails in the Adirondacks

The Adirondack Reader

Views from on High: Fire Tower Trails in the Adirondacks and Catskills

Winterwise: A Backpacker's Guide

FOREST PRESERVE SERIES

Adirondack Trails: High Peaks Region
Adirondack Trails: Northern Region
Adirondack Trails: Central Region
Adirondack Trails: Northville-Placid Trail
Adirondack Trails: West-Central Region
Adirondack Trails: Eastern Region
Adirondack Trails: Southern Region
Catskill Trails: Catskill Region

MAPS

Trails of the Adirondack High Peaks Region
Trails of the Adirondack Northern Region
Trails of the Adirondack Central Region
Northville-Placid Trail
Trails of the Adirondack West-Central Region
Trails of the Adirondack Eastern Region
Trails of the Adirondack Southern Region

ADIRONDACK MOUNTAIN CLUB CALENDAR

Price list available on request

Index

Locations are indexed by proper name, with Camp, Lake, Mount or Mountain following.

A

Adirondack Forest Preserve 13–16
Adirondack Mountain Club
  183-187
Adirondack region, 14–15
Adirondack State Park, 15–16
Auger Falls Trail
  East, 32–33
    map 34
  West, 110–111
    map 34
Austin Falls Walk, 111

B

Bailey Pond Trail, 164, 166
  map, 165
Balance Rock, 161
Baldface Mt. Trail, 94–95
Balm of Gilead Mt. Trail, 56
  map, 54
bears
  hunting season for, 26–27
  safety tips about, 27
beaver fever, 25–26
Big Bad Luck Pond, 84
  map, 85
Blue Ledges Trail, 147–148
blue line, 15

Blue Mountain Lake section,
  123–124
  Blue Mountain Lake from
    South Castle Rock Trail,
    134, 136
  Blue Mt. Trail, 138–139
  Cascade Pond Trail, 131–132
  North Castle Rock Trail, 134,
    136–137
  Rock Lake Trail, 126–127
  Rock River Trail, 125–127
  Sawyer Mt. Trail, 124–126
  South Castle Rock Trail,
    134–136
  Stephens Pond via N-P Trail,
    130–131
  Tirrell Pond and N-P Trail to
    Long Lake, 127–130
  Tirrell Pond from Blue Mt.
    Trailhead, 137–138
  Upper Sargent Pond Trail,
    133–135
  Wilson Pond Trail, 132–133
Bog Meadow Trail, 45–46
Boreas River Trail, 150
Botheration Pond, East Branch
  Sacandaga Trail toward, 60
Bullhead Pond Trail, 81
  map, 82
bushwhacks, 30

C

Callahan Brook Trail, 114–115
camping, 21–24, 179
  Baldface Mt. Trail, 94
  Bog Meadow Trail, 45-46
  Boreas River Trail, 150
  Cheney Pond and Lester Flow, 169
  Cisco Creek Trail to the Kunjamuk River, 104
  Clear Pond Trail, 77
  Elizabeth Point Trail, 58
  Hour Pond Trail, 62
  John Pond Trail, 74
  Mason Lake, 114
  Moose River Recreation Area, 98, 100
  Peaked Mt. Pond and Peaked Mt. Trail, 53
  Pillsbury Lake to West Canada Creek Trail, 122
  Pillsbury Lake Trail, 118
  Puffer Pond Trail, 61
  Rock Pond and Long Pond Trail, 105
  Roosevelt Truck Trail, 170
  Ross Pond Trail, 86
  Santanoni Preserve, 156
  Shanty Brook and Mud Ponds Trail, 38
  Stephens Pond via N-P Trail, 130
  Tirrell Pond and N-P Trail to Long Lake, 129
  Upper Sargent Pond Trail, 133
  Vanderwhacker Mt. Trail, 151
  see also lean-tos

Cartier, Jacques, 14–15
Cascade Pond Trail, 131–132
Cave, Kunjamuk, 102–103
Cedar Lakes Trail, 116–118
  map, 120–121
cell phones, 24
Center Pond Trail, Olmsted-Newcomb, 144
Center Pond Trail, Siamese Ponds, 77–78
  map, 75
Central Region
  boundaries of, 9, 16
  overview maps, 6–7
Champlain, Samuel de, 15
Charles Lathrop Pack Demonstration Forest, 9–10
Nature Trail, 171–174
Cheney Pond and Lester Flow, 168–170
Chimney Mt. Trail, 64–65
Cisco Creek Trail to the Kunjamuk River, 104
Clear Pond Trail, 77
  map, 75
County Line Brook Trail, 33, 35–36
cross country skiing, *see* skiing
Crotched Pond Trail, 93–94
Curtis Clearing Trail, 43–44

D

DEC (Department of Environmental Conservation)
  24-hour telephone hotline, 25
  camping regulations, 21–23

DEC *(continued)*
office addresses, 19–20, 25
origins of, 141
deer ticks, 29
drinking water safety, 23, 25–26
Dug Mt. Brook Falls Trail, 86

E
East Branch Sacandaga
Gorge and Square Falls Trail,
40–41
From Old Farm Clearing Trail,
58–60
To Old Farm Clearing Trail,
41–42
Trail toward Botheration Pond
60
Elizabeth Point Trail, 58
emergency procedures, 25.
See also safety issues

F
falls, *see* waterfalls
fire safety, 22, 23
fire towers, 10
Blue Mt., 139
Goodnow Mt., 157–159
Gore Mt., 50
Pillsbury Mt., 115–116
Snowy Mt., 91
Vanderwhacker Mt., 151, 153,
154
Wakely Mt., 97–98
fishing
Bullhead Pond Trail, 81
Upper Sargent Pond Trail, 133

Forest Preserve, *see* Adirondack
Forest Preserve
forest rangers, contacting of,
23–24
DEC addresses, 19–20, 25
Fox Lair Walk, 39
French Louie, 116

G
Garnet Hill Lodge, 55
garnet mines
Hooper Mine Trail, 56–57
Humphrey Mt. Trail, 69
Peaked Mt. Pond and Peaked
Mt. Trail, 53
Giardia lamblia, 25–26
Glossary of terms, 178
Goodnow Mt., 157, 159
map, 158
Gore Mt. (Schaefer Trail), 47,
49–50
map, 48
Grandmother's Tree, 171, 174
Greene, Don, 47

H
Hayes Flow Trail, 106, 108
map, 107
herd paths, 30
Hewitt Eddy Trail, 151
Hewitt Pond Trail, Stony Pond
from, 143–144
Hoffman Notch Trail, 162–164
map, 165
Hooper Mine Trail, 56–57
map, 54

Hour Pond Trail, 62
Hudnut estate, 39
Hudson, Henry, 15
Hudson River Recreation Area,
  174, 177
  map, 175
Humphrey Mt. Trail, 69
hunting season, 26–27

I

Indian Lake section, 79–81
  Baldface Mt. Trail, 94–95
  Big Bad Luck Pond, 84–85
  Bullhead Pond Trail, 81–82
  Crotched Pond Trail, 93–94
  Dug Mt. Brook Falls Trail, 86
  John Mack Pond-Long Pond
    Cross Trail, 92–93
  John Mack Pond Trail, 91–92
  Moose River Recreation Area,
    98, 100
  Northville-Placid Trail from
    Wakely Dam, 96, 99, 100
  Ross Pond Trail, 84–86
  Snowy Mt. Trail, 90–91
  Sprague Pond Trail, 95–96
  Stephens Pond from McCanes,
    96–97
  Sucker Brook Trail, 87–88, 157
  Wakely Mt. Trail, 97–99
  Watch Hill from Indian Lake
    Trail, 89–90
  Watch Hill from NY 30 Trail,
    88–89
  Whortleberry Pond Trail, 81,
    83, 85

International Paper Company, 10
  land use policies, 63, 70
  permits required by, 101
  Speculator office of, 101
Irishtown Trail, Stony Pond from,
  145–147

J

Jessup River Trail and Panther
  Pond, 113
John Mack Pond Trail, 91–92
  –Long Pond Cross Trail, 92–93
John Pond Trail, 73–74, 76
  Crossover Trail, 75–76
  map 75

K

Kings Flow
  East Trail, 68
  Puffer Pond from, 66–67
Kunjamuk Cave, 102–103
Kunjamuk Mt. Trail, 73
Kunjamuk section, 101–102
  Cisco Creek Trail to the
    Kunjamuk River, 104
  Hayes Flow Trail, 106–108
  Kunjamuk Cave, 102–103
  Lower Pine Lakes Trail,
    103–104
  Rock Pond and Long Pond
    Trail, 105–106
Kunjamuk Trail, 70–72
  Round Pond from, 72–73

L

lean-tos, 21, 22, 23
  Cascade Pond Trail, 131
  East Branch Sacandaga to Old
    Farm Clearing Trail, 42
  East Branch Sacandaga Trail
    from Old Farm Clearing
    Trail, 59
  John Pond Trail, 74
  Pillsbury Lake to West Canada
    Creek Trail, 122
  Pillsbury Lake Trail, 118
  Puffer Pond Trail, 61
  Siamese Ponds Trail, 44
  Stephens Pond from McCanes,
    97
  Stephens Pond via N-P Trail,
    130
  Stony Pond from Hewitt Pond
    Trail, 144
  Stony Pond from NY 28N, 145
  Tirrell Pond and N-P Trail to
    Long Lake, 128
  Wilson Pond Trail, 132
Leave No Trace program, 28
Lester Flow and Cheney Pond,
  168–169
Lewey Lake, *see* Wells to Lewey
  Lake section
Linsey Marsh Trail, 149–150
logging, 9–11, 15
Long Lake, Tirrell Pond and N-P
  Trail to, 127–130
Long Pond Trail and Rock Pond,
  105–106
Lower Pine Lakes Trail, 103–104

Lyme disease, 29

M

Mason Lake Campsites, 114
mines, *see* garnet mines
Moose River Recreation Area,
  98, 100
mosquitoes, 29
Mud Ponds Trail and Shanty
  Brook, 36–38

N

Newcomb Visitor Interpretive
  Center, 156–157
North Castle Rock Trail, 136–137
  map, 134
Northeast section, 161–162
  Bailey Pond Trail, 164–166
  Cheney Pond and Lester Flow,
    168–169
  Hoffman Notch Trail, 162–165
  Roosevelt Truck Trail, 170
  Severance (Mt.) Trail, 166–168
Northville-Placid Trail
  Stephens Pond via, 130–131
  Tirrell Pond to Long Lake and,
    127–130
  Wakely Dam to, 96, 100
  map, 99

O

Old Farm Clearing Trail, 57–58
  East Branch Sacandaga to,
    41–42
  East Branch Sacandaga Trail
    from, 58–60

Olmsted-Newcomb section,
141–142
Blue Ledges Trail, 147–148
Boreas River Trail, 150
Center Pond Trail, 144
Goodnow Mt., 157–159
Hewitt Eddy Trail, 151
Linsey Marsh Trail, 149–150
Newcomb Visitor Interpretive
Center, 156–157
Rankin Pond Trail, 149
Santanoni Preserve, 154–156
Stony Pond Country, 142
Stony Pond from Hewitt Pond
Trail, 143–144
Stony Pond from Irishtown
Trail, 145–147
Stony Pond from NY 28N, 145
Vanderwhacker Mt. Trail,
151–154
Oregon Tannery, 39

P
Palmer Pond Trail, 177
map, 176
Panther Pond and Jessup River
Trail, 113
Peaked Mt. Pond and Peaked Mt.
Trail, 52–53, 55
Peninsula Forest Primeval Trail,
157
permits, required for camping
by DEC, 21–22, 23–24
by International Paper
Company, 101
pets, 22

Pillsbury Lake
Trail, 118, 120–121
West Canada Creek Trail from,
119, 120–122
Pillsbury Mt., 115–116
map, 120–121
Puffer Pond
Brook Trail, 67
Kings Flow Trail, 66–67
Trail, 61–62

R
rabies, 29
rafting, 147
rangers, contacting of, 23–24
DEC addresses, 19–20, 25
Rankin Pond Trail, 149
Rich Lake Trail, 157
Rock Lake Trail, 127
map, 126
Rock Pond and Long Pond Trail,
105–106
Rock River Trail, 125, 127
map, 126
Roosevelt, Theodore, 10
Roosevelt Truck Trail, 170
Ross Pond Trail, 84, 86
map, 85
Round Pond from Kunjamuk
Trail, 72–73

S
Sacandaga River, *see* East Branch
Sacandaga River
safety issues
bears, 26–27

safety issues *(continued)*
  emergency procedures, 25
  fires, 22, 23
  hunting season, 26–27
  mosquitoes, 29
  navigation in woods, 24
  rabies, 29
  ranger contact information,
    23–24, 25
  ticks, 29
  water, 23, 25–26
  weather, 24–25
Santanoni Preserve, 154, 156
  map, 155
Sawyer Mt. Trail, 124–125
  map, 126
Schaefer brothers, 47
Schaefer Trail, 47, 49–50
  map, 48
Second Pond Trail, 46–47
Severance (Mt.) Trail, 166, 168
  map, 167
Shanty Brook and Mud Ponds
  Trail, 36–38
shelters, *see* lean-tos
Siamese Ponds, from the east,
  51–52
  Balm of Gilead Mt. Trail, 54, 56
  East Branch Sacandaga Trail
    from Old Farm Clearing
    Trail, 58–60
  East Branch Sacandaga Trail
    toward Botheration Pond, 60
  Elizabeth Point Trail, 58
  Hooper Mine Trail, 54, 56–57
  Hour Pond Trail, 62

  Old Farm Clearing Trail, 57–58
  Peaked Mt. Pond and Peaked
    Mt. Trail, 52–53, 55
  Puffer Pond Trail, 61–62
  William Blake Pond Trail, 54, 55
Siamese Ponds, from the north,
  63–64
  Center Pond Trail, 75, 77–78
  Chimney Mt. Trail, 64–65
  Clear Pond Trail, 75, 77
  Humphrey Mt. Trail, 69
  John Pond Crossover Trail, 75, 76
  John Pond Trail, 73–76
  Kings Flow East Trail, 68
  Kunjamuk Trail, 70–72
  Kunjamuk Mt. Trail, 73
  Puffer Pond Brook Trail, 67
  Puffer Pond from Kings Flow
    Trail, 66–67
  Round Pond from Kunjamuk
    Trail, 72–73
Siamese Ponds, from the south,
  31–32
  Auger Falls East Trail, 32–33, 34
  Bog Meadow Trail, 45–46
  County Line Brook Trail, 33,
    35–36
  Curtis Clearing Trail, 43–44
  East Branch Sacandaga Gorge
    and Square Falls Trail, 40–41
  East Branch Sacandaga Trail
    to Old Farm Clearing Trail,
    41–42
  Fox Lair Walk, 39
  Gore Mt. (Schaefer Trail),
    47–50

Second Pond Trail, 46–47
Shanty Brook and Mud Ponds
   Trail, 36–39
Siamese Ponds Trail, 44
skiing
  Auger Falls East Trail, 33
  Bailey Pond Trail, 166
  Big Bad Luck Pond, 84
  Blue Mountain Lake from
     South Castle Rock Trail, 136
  Bog Meadow Trail, 46
  Cedar Lakes Trail, 117
  Cheney Pond and Lester Flow,
     168–169
  Cisco Creek Trail to the
     Kunjamuk River, 104
  Clear Pond Trail, 77
  County Line Brook Trail, 36
  East Branch Sacandaga Gorge
     to Old Farm Clearing Trail, 42
  East Branch Sacandaga Trail
     from Old Farm Clearing Trail,
     60
  East Branch Sacandaga Trail
     toward Botheration Pond, 60
  Elizabeth Point Trail, 58
  Garnet Hill Lodge, 55
  Gore Mt. (Schaefer Trail),
     47, 49–50
  Hoffman Notch Trail, 164
  Hooper Mine Trail, 57
  Hudson River Recreation
     Area, 174, 177
  John Pond Trail, 76
  Kings Flow East Trail, 68
  Kunjamuk Trail, 72

Linsey Marsh Trail, 150
Old Farm Clearing Trail, 57
Palmer Pond Trail, 177
Pillsbury Lake Trail, 118
Pillsbury Lake to West Canada
   Creek Trail, 122
Puffer Pond Brook Trail, 67
Puffer Pond from Kings Flow
   Trail, 66, 67
Roosevelt Truck Trail, 170
Round Pond from Kunjamuk
   Trail, 72
Second Pond Trail, 47
Shanty Brook and Mud Ponds
   Trail, 38
Siamese Ponds Trail, 44
Stephens Pond via N-P Trail,
   131
Stony Pond from NY 28N, 145
Tirrell Pond and N-P Trail to
   Long Lake, 130
Tirrell Pond from Blue Mt.
   Trailhead, 138
Vanderwhacker Mt. Trail, 154
Watch Hill from NY 30 Trail, 89
Whortleberry Pond Trail, 83
William Blake Pond Trail, 55
snowshoeing
  Balm of Gilead Mt. Trail, 56
  Blue Mountain Lake from
     South Castle Rock Trail, 136
  Bog Meadow Trail, 46
  Bullhead Pond Trail, 81
  Cedar Lakes Trail, 117
  Center Pond Trail, Olmsted-
     Newcomb, 144

snowshoeing *(continued)*
  Center Pond Trail, Siamese
    Ponds, 78
  Chimney Mt. Trail, 65
  Fox Lair Walk, 39
  Goodnow Mt., 159
  Gore Mt. (Schaefer Trail), 50
  Hewitt Eddy Trail, 151
  Hoffman Notch Trail, 164
  Hooper Mine Trail, 57
  Hudson River Recreation Area,
    174, 177
  Humphrey Mt. Trail, 69
  Kings Flow East Trail, 68
  Linsey Marsh Trail, 150
  Newcomb Visitor Interpretive
    Center, 157
  Palmer Pond Trail, 177
  Peaked Mt. Pond and Peaked
    Mt. Trail, 53
  Pillsbury Lake to West Canada
    Creek Trail, 122
  Pillsbury Mt., 116
  Puffer Pond from Kings Flow
    Trail, 66
  Ross Pond Trail, 86
  Sawyer Mt. Trail, 125
  Severance (Mt.) Trail, 168
  Snowy Mt. Trail, 91
  Vanderwhacker Mt. Trail, 154
  Watch Hill from NY 30 Trail,
    88
  Whortleberry Pond Trail, 83
Snowy Mt. Trail, 90–91
South Castle Rock Trail, 135–136
  Blue Mountain Lake from, 136

map, 134
Southeast section, 171
  Charles Lathrop Pack
    Demonstration Forest 9–10,
    Nature Trail, 171–174
  Hudson River Recreation
    Area, 174–175, 177
  Palmer Pond Trail, 176, 177
Speculator Tree Farm, 101
Sprague Pond Trail, 95
  map, 96
Square Falls Trail and East Branch
  Sacandaga Gorge, 40–41
State campgrounds, 179
Stephens Pond
  McCanes to, 96–97
  via N-P Trail, 130–131
Stony Pond
  Hewitt Pond Trail to, 143–144
  Irishtown Trail to, 145–147
  NY 28N to, 145
Stony Pond Country, 142
Sucker Brook Trail, 87–88, 157

T
tannery, 39
telephones
  cellular, 24
  emergency numbers for, 25
ticks, 29
timber, *see* logging
Tirrell Pond
  Blue Mt. Trailhead to, 137–138
  N-P Trail to Long Lake and,
    127–130

trails
  bushwhacks, 30
  changes in condition of, 11
  distance and time for, 20–21
  herd paths, 30
  markers for, 17–19
  on private land, 20
  unmaintained, 29–30

U
Upper Sargent Pond Trail, 133,
    135
  map, 134

V
Vanderwhacker Mt. Trail,
    151–152, 154
  map, 153

W
Wakely Mt. Trail, 97–98
  map, 99
waste disposal, 22
Watch Hill
  Indian Lake Trail to, 89–90
  NY 30 Trail to, 88–89
waterfalls
  Auger Falls, 33
  Austin Falls, 111
  County Line Brook Falls, 35
  Dug Mt. Brook Falls, 86
  Griffin Falls, 33
  Shanty Brook Falls, 37
  Stony Pond from Irishtown
    Trail, 146
water safety, 23, 25–26

weather safety, 24–25
Wells to Lewey Lake section,
    109–110
  Auger Falls (West) Trail, 34,
    110–111
  Austin Falls Walk, 111
  Callahan Brook Trail, 114–115
  Cedar Lakes Trail, 116–118,
    120–121
  Mason Lake Campsites, 114
  Panther Pond and Jessup River
    Trail, 113
  Pillsbury Lake to West Canada
    Creek Trail, 119–122
  Pillsbury Lake Trail, 118,
    120–121
  Pillsbury Mt., 115–116,
    120–121
West Canada Creek Trail from
    Pillsbury Lake, 119, 122
  map, 120–121
West Nile Virus, 29
Whortleberry Pond Trail, 81, 83
  map, 85
William Blake Pond Trail, 55
  map, 54
Wilson Pond Trail, 132–133
winter travel, 24–25

Notes

Notes

Notes